Advance Praise fo

M000306547

"With her book *The Millionairess Mentality,* Tamar Hermes demystifies real estate investing for women everywhere—providing them with one of the most powerful tools for wealth and financial independence in the process."

LIZ FAIRCLOTH, COFOUNDER OF THE DEROSA GROUP AND *THE REAL ESTATE INVESTHER* PODCAST AND COMMUNITY

"Tamar Hermes understands what it takes to be successful in real estate, and with this book, she generously explains all the ins and outs in terms anyone can understand. *The Millionairess Mentality* is sure to change a lot of women's lives."

JUSTIN DONALD, ENTREPRENEUR, INVESTOR AND #1 *WALL STREET JOURNAL* AND *USA TODAY* BESTSELLING AUTHOR OF *THE LIFESTYLE INVESTOR*

"*The Millionairess Mentality* is a true gift to women looking to master real estate investing. All financial savvy aside, Tamar Hermes's book proves that she is dedicated to helping women achieve the lives of their dreams."

DAVID OSBORN, *NEW YORK TIMES* BESTSELLING AUTHOR OF *WEALTH CAN'T WAIT, TRIBE OF MILLIONAIRES, BIDDING TO BUY* AND *MIRACLE MORNING MILLIONAIRES*

"Tamar Hermes's book breaks the complicated subject of real estate investing into digestible, pragmatic pieces. *The Millionairess Mentality* belongs on the shelves of entrepreneurial women everywhere."

KRISTIN MARQUET, CREATIVE DIRECTOR AND CEO OF MARQUET MEDIA AND FEMFOUNDER.CO, *ENTREPRENEUR* CONTRIBUTING WRITER

"Real estate investing and wealth building don't have to be things that other people do. They are things that anyone, from anywhere, can do—and in *The Millionairess Mentality,* Tamar Hermes proves that by walking the walk and blazing a path for other women."

AVERY CARL, CEO AND FOUNDER OF THE SHORT TERM SHOP

THE MILLIONAIRESS MENTALITY

A PROFESSIONAL WOMAN'S GUIDE TO BUILDING WEALTH THROUGH REAL ESTATE

TAMAR HERMES

ISBN: 978-1-956955-27-9 ebook

ISBN: 978-1-956955-28-6 paperback

DISCLAIMER

Please read this: The author has done her best to provide useful and accurate information about real estate investing, but please be aware that there are no guarantees, and there are many variables specific to any given situation that she cannot anticipate. Readers are responsible for researching all material and tips herein themselves before relying upon them. Therefore, the author makes no guarantees of outcome concerning the information in this book. In the event readers use any of the information in this book, the author and publisher assume no responsibility for their actions.

All the proceeds of this book will be donated to MONA Foundation. For over 20 years, MONA has supported the education and development of gender equality for women in the poorest and most forgotten parts of the world. To learn more about MONA Foundation, visit *www.mon-afoundation.org*. Imagine how educating just one woman impacts the lives of one hundred more over time. Every dollar invested in education equals $10 in economic growth.

CONTENTS

To all the women in the world who are overwhelmed and fearful that having a life of financial freedom isn't accessible, may this book provide them the tools and confidence needed to kick those limiting thoughts to the curb and fearlessly build their financial dreams

FOREWORD

I'm not sure where I became friends with Tamar Hermes —maybe it was through a real estate investing forum (probably Bigger Pockets). She reached out one day, jumped in and decided we were friends. I complied—not because I *had to,* but because her energy was infectious. Even before I knew much about Tamar, I could tell she was the real deal and that she was doing big things.

I was considering joining the *GoBundance Women's Tribe* and had just submitted my application. I was waiting to hear back when I was on the phone with Tamar about something else and mentioned my pending application.

"Oh!" she said. "I joined recently, too! Let me check on your application and make sure that you get into my pod."

And that was that. I have been friends with Tamar, talking almost daily, for the three years since.

When Tamar and I met, I didn't really know many other women who were real estate investors. I had one or two friends who had started as past clients and eventually ended up working for me at my company The Short Term Shop, but those friends were on the exact same investing path as me: they had started at nearly the exact same time and were making the exact same investments in the same way that I was.

What excited me about Tamar was that she was doing *different* things than I was, and she was successful at them. It was such a breath of fresh air to meet another woman who was out there digging in the dirt and finding different ways to build her portfolio. I have always been impressed by Tamar's ability to jump into things and learn as she goes.

One day, I told Tamar about a new short-term rental cabin development in Sevierville, Tennessee that I had coming up off-market. Without even a fraction of a second of hesitation, Tamar said, "I want one—where do I sign?" She still doesn't have her cabin yet (because new construction never finishes on time), but she is hanging in there (I am chuckling because as of this writing, she's been waiting 18 months). The point is, Tamar's not afraid of a new asset class, and she's willing to take risks. (Like being my instant friend—do you see the pattern yet?)

It has been really cool to watch Tamar advance her

career at every turn over the few years I have known her. Maybe she was always the most connected woman in real estate, and I just wasn't aware—but since we've been friends, I feel like she has *really* become the most connected woman in real estate. She knows *everyone*. I have never seen anyone so fearless, anyone so willing to jump into friendships with strangers (there's the "jumping in" theme again). When it comes to the big players, whether in self-storage or short-term rentals or multifamily, Tamar has them in her phone—and she's probably talked to them at some point this week (meanwhile, the rest of us are still only thinking about calling them).

These traits are important to mention because Tamar wasn't born into a real estate empire, nor was she born into privilege. Her connections are not people she grew up with. Her investments were not inherited. Before building her wealth, she was a woman, like many of us, who was in a completely different field and on a completely different career trajectory.

Tamar had the courage to leap—to find a better way to earn and build, and to teach herself how to develop her business so that she wasn't at the mercy of a boss. That's what I find so special about her and what I think most people will find to be the most important takeaway from this book.

No one is born into being successful at real estate investing. No one starts at the finish line, but no matter where you start, you have to have the mindset and willingness to jump in and navigate from point A to point B. Real estate investing and wealth building don't have to be things that other people do. They are things that anyone, from anywhere, can do—and in *The Millionairess Mentality,* Tamar proves that by walking the walk and blazing a path for other women.

I think Tamar is a brilliant example of success, and this book is an excellent place for people to gain the confidence to begin their own journey.

Avery Carl
CEO and Founder of
The Short Term Shop

AUTHOR'S NOTE

One of the reasons I wrote this book was that I couldn't find one resource and one place that clearly explained all the options I could pursue in real estate investing. Where you focus your efforts and how much energy you invest will depend largely on personal factors including budget, time and risk tolerance, but in this book, I intend to give you the full range. I will show you ways to do almost no work or a lot of work. I will explain managing partnerships and managing your own portfolio privately. There is no one size that fits all.

Before you dive in, I created a quiz to help you discover your real estate personality based on the factors noted above and get a sense of where you are in the real estate investing process.

To take it, go to tamarquiz.com or scan the QR code below to get a head start on narrowing your focus.

Over the course of your real estate investing journey, you will pivot and expand. It's an exciting process that begins with this first step, so complete the quiz below now —and then start reading!

INTRODUCTION

> *Women often don't want to know about real estate because it overwhelms them, but the ones who learn it make a ton of money.*
> —Tamar Hermes

It was the fourth time I had cried on the floor of my office that week. To anyone looking at my life from the outside, it must have seemed like I had it made. After all, I was a 28-year-old executive in the entertainment industry making well over six figures a year. I had a great job with lots of creative freedom and supportive colleagues. What right did I have to complain?

The reality was I simply wasn't happy. Life had become more of a chore than a joy. Despite the perks, my job also meant long hours and stressful assignments with tight deadlines. I longed for something with more flexibility—a life that didn't require waking up early every morning and heading into an office. I felt lost and trapped, because I didn't know what else I could do to maintain my lifestyle, the one that allowed me to travel, pay my bills and enjoy nice meals out with friends.

That feeling of being trapped was familiar; I'd felt it my entire life. My parents weren't great communicators and never shared encouraging messages like, "You can do anything you want in your life," or, "It doesn't matter how much money you have." When I was growing up, we always had just enough money to get by, and life was explained to me as hard and unfair.

As I grew up and entered the workforce, I watched as my friends navigated their careers with a clear roadmap of what they wanted to do to earn a living. My path remained hazy, though certainly, all my options seemed to involve working for someone else. I never thought I could be competent enough to have my own business.

Instead, I believed I should count my blessings that I was making such a good living since I simply wasn't capable of anything else—or, God forbid, anything *more*. It was a limiting belief that hurt me more than anything else in my life.

I didn't even feel like I chose my career. I never had a sense of *why* I was doing anything. While I now know that this thinking was an illusion, it felt like I was floating down a river with no control of where the water would take me.

I always assumed that money or a new relationship would fix what was broken in my life and heal my feelings of confusion, but those things only served as Band-Aids at best. The good news was that I had learned one thing I *didn't* want: to head to a job every day for the rest of my life. My problem was that I simply didn't know what I wanted.

Being dumped was the final straw that brought me to my knees on my office floor, crying in despair. After three years of living together, the guy I thought I would marry decided I wasn't the one after all, and he walked out on me. Suddenly, reality seeped in: I had no true purpose, and the thought of working for money alone for the rest of my life felt unbearable.

I wanted to find a way out, but there was no *Eat, Pray, Love* story for me. I was too plagued by my fear of losing my paycheck. I couldn't lean on my parents either; their lack of parenting skills was a result of their own hardships. My father was a Holocaust survivor, and my mom grew up in a kibbutz in Palestine before it became the land of Israel. They were both masters at survival, but they didn't have much vision beyond that. They resigned themselves to a life of scraping by, and even though I had managed to elevate myself to a six-figure salary, I was stuck following their pattern.

Survival for them was a victory, and I absolutely honor where they came from. But I grew up in America, where I could imagine so much more than mere survival. In America, I could *thrive*. I knew there was more, and I wanted it. I just had no clue how to get it.

I definitely didn't see money as the solution to all my problems, but continually needing to prioritize it felt like a tremendous burden. I'd gotten a taste of what having money could do in life: I had traveled to Guatemala and Europe, paid my bills without worry, had a cute apartment in a hip area of Los Angeles, bought organic produce and regularly donated to charity. There was a lot to be said for those pleasures and luxuries. I knew some people had a lot more money than I did, but those were lives meant for only the lucky few, weren't they? This daily stream of thoughts was constantly cluttering my mind.

I was determined to find a way to own my time and do what I wanted in my life. If I didn't need to focus so much on making money, surely I could discover my true desires and find a way to live a life of luxury and give back to others.

My First Investment

At the time, I lived in the cutest little group of five bungalows. The property owner also worked in television, and each month, I wrote him a check for $750. Meanwhile, my friend next door paid him $1,000 for a slightly larger unit. I couldn't help but wonder how I could get on my landlord's side of the equation—becoming the person who received the checks instead of the person who wrote them month after month.

If I could stop paying rent, my highest monthly expense, I could lower my burden, I thought. *And if I could have my own tenant, I could start collecting those checks.*

I began calling realtors in the area and told them I wanted to buy my first property. Suddenly, I had a purpose, a direction and a plan—a potential way out of my financial trap. As I looked at properties, I definitely felt nervous, but I was determined to take the leap, however small.

After a few months, I found a duplex that felt right and already had a tenant in place. I held my breath and made an offer. Back in those days (more than 20 years ago), properties were not in multiple offers, and it was a much easier time to purchase. But it was still scary. I spent more money on that one transaction than I'd ever spent on anything, and the people around me kept telling me that owning real estate was risky. I had to sign a ton of documents I didn't fully understand, and I couldn't project how difficult the tenant would be or if there would be unforeseeable expenses with the property. Yikes!

Still, even with all of the uncertainties and the as-yet-unresolved mental anguish over the meaning of my life, I felt a great sense of accomplishment. I had taken bold action, and I instinctively felt I was on my way to solving one of my big quandaries in life. As long as I never defaulted on my loan, the property would be mine.

Still, as I watched the property values grow and collected my tenant's rent check, all those negative thoughts and worries about what could go wrong flooded my mind. Though I was seeing the incredible results of my purchase, I did not buy more property. I simply had no idea how to build upon my investment and was quite frankly too scared—what if I had just gotten lucky the first time?

It took a few years for me to gather the courage to buy a second duplex, taking on two more tenants and starting to build a portfolio. Buying the second property wasn't as challenging, but I was still riddled with fear and dozens of questions that could only be answered through trial, error and many costly mistakes.

For years, I chose complacency instead of rocking the boat by dreaming too big. I bought properties very slowly and played it safe. Even as I became financially free, I constantly questioned my decisions and what I understood about real estate investing.

Over time, I learned how to grow wealth through buying and selling as well as partnering and investing in real estate, but I could have gotten there sooner if only I'd had a roadmap and support when I started. If I had learned how to change my mindset along the way, I could have avoided many of the mistakes I made. I could have built on my first purchase much faster and reached my current level of success with fewer challenges and less fear.

I'm assuming that if you picked up this book, you're a woman who's tired of the money struggle. You're ready to step into your power, and you're wondering if buying real estate is a good idea for you. I wrote this book with *you* in mind. This book is the roadmap and support I wish I'd had early in my investing career. It's meant to spare you the mistakes I made so that you can reap the benefits much sooner and without the growing pains I experienced.

I understand that you may still be somewhat skeptical and fearful. You may have heard that there is only one way to invest in real estate, and you might have already decided that way doesn't work for you. Don't worry—this book will prove that there isn't just one way to build a real estate investment portfolio. I'll open your mind to new ideas and different avenues of possibility, and once you understand the process of how money and real estate work, you'll have the confidence to take action. You'll take responsibility for your financial life and trust yourself enough to make educated decisions.

As you work through this book, buying and investing in property won't feel so overwhelming. You'll no longer be on the journey alone. I will serve as your initial partner and guide while you read, and I'll show you how to find partners for every part of the investing process.

You'll discover the many options you have for investing so that you won't miss out on great opportunities.

You'll find out that the industry is so forgiving that if you own a property long enough, you'll generally make good money. Even if you lose some along the way, you'll likely gain more in the long run. You'll learn that losing money isn't even something to fear. You'll discover that there's always another opportunity and that money is inherently meant to move, not remain stagnant.

Of course, you may choose to invest at a more gradual pace to meet your risk tolerance and comfort level. I want you to honor that within yourself and keep on moving without judging yourself for it. You only need to do the work and grow a healthy financial mindset, and I'll help you with both. When you finish reading, you'll know how to confidently stand up to the limitations you have created around your ability to become wealthy.

Over the years, I have hired many coaches to support me, and I'll share all the knowledge I gained from these experts. As you explore the financial life you want and define how much action you're willing to take to get it, you'll find that your success is ultimately your choice. I define "financial freedom" as the number that allows me the lifestyle I want without having to go to work another day in my life. If that sounds good to you, this book will show you how to find that magic number and meet it.

Nevertheless, this isn't a "get rich quick" book. Some of the self-proclaimed "real estate gurus" out there will tell you it can happen overnight, but I want to set you on a stable path to a sustainable life of wealth. Building a portfolio is a process of calculated investments, so you must understand how to live and work with money.

Nothing great is accomplished without effort. So yes, I'm still challenged, and every investment has its risks and unknowns. But I'm also able to manage and mitigate those risks through the knowledge I'll share with you as you continue reading.

As you move through these comprehensive chapters, you'll place yourself on an exciting path that can fulfill your dream of no longer exchanging your time for money. Your real estate assets will support you, and working to earn money won't be the top priority in your life. You'll build a legacy and be able to look back at your life and say, "I lived fully."

So grab a notebook and a pen, and let's get started.

ONE
IT'S OKAY TO WANT MONEY

> *Money can't buy happiness, but it can make you awfully comfortable while you're being miserable.*
> —Clare Boothe Luce

From age 10 to 13, I slept on a pullout sofa next to my sister in my grandparents' living room. My parents were getting a divorce, and my mom had no money and no easy way to earn it.

After my mom finally landed a job as a bookkeeper, she managed to save up enough money to move us into an apartment. While I'm grateful to have had a roof over my head, the apartment was built with cinderblocks and had a tiny kitchen, three bedrooms and no yard. There was no grass nor any trees on my street. My window faced the wall of another unit that looked just like mine, and we got robbed more than once (luckily, we were never home when it happened).

Those feelings of instability, lack and victimization became my internal reality. I truly believed that money wasn't for me because I grew up poor. I felt guilty for even wanting more money, because I thought feeling that way meant that I was greedy and ungrateful for what I had.

I would come home from school every day to find a pan of chicken with potatoes that my mother had left for us in the oven. My sister and I did our homework, went to bed and did it all again the next day. Sometimes, I would watch soap operas and get lost in the world on the screen. I felt so pathetic, small and lost. I had no idea how I would ever create a different reality than the world that enveloped me.

My mom wanted us to have a good education, so she found a friend who lived in Beverly Hills and used their address to get us into schools in that district. My new school friends had fancy cars and houses, and they went on exotic vacations. I would go home to my sad apartment, bewildered that my wealthy friends came into this world with so much while my family had so little.

I believed where my parents came from dictated my lot in life. Because he was Jewish, my father spent three years in a concentration camp and later moved to a work camp during World War II. At 14 years old, his job was to bury dead people. If he hadn't done the work, he would've been killed on the spot. He lost his mom and sister, and his father was wracked with guilt that he didn't leave Romania before the Nazis enslaved all the Jews. He then took his anger out on my father.

My mother's childhood was also stressful. She grew up in the 1950s on a kibbutz in Palestine, where her parents fought for the land to be declared the State of Israel. She spent her childhood with Syrians shooting at her and the other families from the hillside, causing all the children to race to barracks for cover.

For both of my parents, freedom meant waking up in the morning and not having a gun pointed at their heads. Survival was the goal of their childhood, and it was a mentality they carried into adulthood. I lived as they did but felt sad that life felt like a chore and nothing more. Dreaming wasn't something we talked about, and it definitely wasn't something that we did. It felt uncomfortable or even wrong to imagine anything more than what we had.

What's Wrong with Being Rich?

I decided that people with money were better than my family, and I believed they were judging me. So, I judged them. I see now that they weren't looking at me in that way, but at the time, staying small and unassuming felt like the only way to feel safe.

Even though a part of me felt insignificant, I kept showing up for life. I knew my parents wouldn't be able to afford to buy me a car when I turned 16, so when I was 14, I started thinking about all the ways I could get a car by the time I was able to drive. I got my first job as a hostess in a restaurant nearby and managed to save $5,000 by the time I was 16–just enough to get a used Ford Escort. As a result of this personal win, I started to focus less on what I didn't have and more on what I wanted, and I finally realized that wanting money wasn't actually a bad thing.

Most of the kids at Beverly Hills High School were planning on attending college, so I applied as well, selecting the one that gave me the largest scholarship. When I was accepted, Pitzer College in Claremont, California became my entry into new ideas and concepts about the world. I began to understand that my life needed to be defined by much more than what I took away from my childhood. Moving forward, I was going to write my own journey.

I still had no idea what I wanted to do with my life or how to achieve even my small goals, but I started to plant new seeds. I had an interest in art and travel, but if I wanted to see the world, I would need to find a way to make the money to do it. As I waitressed, sold season tickets to the opera and created art pieces for sale, I got more of a taste for having money. I was able to make it, keep some of it and even buy some of the things I wanted.

Women and Money

I'm far from alone in my limiting attitudes about money. After coaching hundreds of women, I've come to see patterns in the way we tend to view money and growing wealth. Real estate investing and most other industries are still dominated by men. Women still earn less and are held back from earning their share—and in some cases, they are holding themselves back.

Chances are you also grew up in an environment where growing wealth wasn't part of your family's conversation. You likely created stories about your ability to earn money and whether that was a noble desire or just greed. By illustrating my own childhood, I'm hoping to show you how these thoughts were falsely imprinted in my mind. If you have any similar feelings around money, it's likely that somewhere along your journey, you too decided that you shouldn't want much, and you believed you were limited in your ability to earn more. I want you to realize that these are beliefs; they are not facts.

Other false notions I've seen over and over again have to do with women's role in society. Many women today are still stuck in the dynamic where most of the money is made by the man. If they make more than their husbands, the men feel inferior, intimidated and jealous. Women also sometimes feel that if they earn too much money, they're taking away from someone else—or if they have too much money, they label themselves as greedy.

The naysayers (mostly people without money) will tell you it's impossible to make more. They'll say you aren't smart enough or that it's too risky to want more. They'll tell you that you have to have money to make money. Of course, it can feel scary to try something new, so it may feel safer sticking with what you know. But that keeps you trapped in a box with no potential for growth. You may also worry that you'll be judged for wanting to be wealthy, or that people around you might say, "All you care about is money." But what's important is that *you* decide what *you* value and want for your life before building the courage to forge ahead.

Over the years, many of my clients have ended up making many multiples of six figures a year only to spend it all frivolously. In many of those cases, they were subconsciously sabotaging their ability to be wealthy. Despite their successes, they still believed that if they didn't choose to buy their Teslas or rare sports cars right away, they might never get another chance to do so in the future. They didn't see that buying real estate would ultimately set them up for life and for generations to come. As readers will see, budgeting and making choices about what to buy now and save for later play a large part in developing the Millionairess Mentality.

If you're still balking at the idea that you can achieve wealth beyond your wildest dreams, ask yourself whether you're willing to live *less* of a life than you want. Are you okay with living paycheck to paycheck, saving every dollar for vacation, feeling guilty if you buy a $6 Starbucks coffee or a new pair of shoes? Are you assuming that the government will support you with social security or that your kids will be able to take care of you in your golden years? If you picked up this book, there's a voice deep inside you that knows how capable you really are. Imagine if you could build your own wealth and also give to charity, start programs to help others and set an example for other women about what is possible for them. Don't you want to be a part of the revolution of women living more prosperous lives?

If you want to stop living hand to mouth, you will need to come to terms with the fact that this life is yours to shape and make into what you want. You'll also need to adjust your idea about wealthy people so that you feel honored and not embarrassed to become one of them. People who grow up without money often decide that rich people are bad and that money is the root of all evil. But isn't that just sour grapes? You don't have to become Jeff Bezos to be wealthy, and there are many wonderful, giving and magnanimous people with wealth.

Once my husband and I were making good money, I could feel myself wanting to pull back. I asked myself how much money I really needed and even worried that if I made too much, I was taking away from someone else. Eventually, I expanded my thinking to envision that there was enough for everyone. Once I realized what I was capable of, I came to believe that every other woman was capable of it as well.

When you think of wealth, you can think about Scrooge or you can envision Oprah and Michelle Obama —philanthropic and generous leaders of the world. You can choose to focus on the good in the world or the bad. It's your choice how you frame your vision. Money is a tool that can help us buy comfortable homes, travel the world, send our kids to college, work if and when we choose and leave a legacy for the next generation. There's no reason to feel guilty about wanting any of that. But money also puts us in a unique position to help others. When a woman makes a million dollars, she sets the stage for other women to follow in her footsteps. You can be that woman.

Money is a tool that affords us many opportunities that have revolutionized the world. Imagine the fact that the dishwasher, fire escape, medical syringe and car heater were all invented by women. Do you think that at some point, those women needed money to test their products and make prototypes? Think how much better these products have made the world and how much money they made.

Once I began seeing the impact I could have on the world and in the lives of other women, I wanted to get as much as I could so that I could help as many people as possible while also creating an enjoyable life for myself and my family.

So many years of my life were wasted feeling defeated and sad. Feeling okay with having money was the first step towards opening up the possibilities that were available to me, and having reasons for wanting the money made all the difference in taking that step.

Knowing Your Why

I'm cringing a little to write this, because "knowing your why" has become a cliché ever since Simon Sinek coined the phrase in a TED Talk he gave (which I recommend if you've never seen it). Still, the idea behind this phrase is that your *why* is at the heart of all that you do, and it's what keeps you motivated and passionate about hanging onto your dreams and aspirations at any cost.

For me, my *why* was my deep desire not to surrender to the hand I was dealt. Embracing this cause led me to self-empowerment and the ability to create a different reality for myself.

So, decide what having money from real estate investing will give you. You may want it so that your family will be taken care of, or so you can live in a great home, travel the world, pay for medical care, have the best education or contribute to a cause or charity that is meaningful to you. Whatever it is for you, declare it as your *why* —or don't even bother with this book.

Taking the action steps outlined in the following chapters will be necessary to help you reach your goals, but it is your determination that will drive you. It's important to make growing wealth through real estate a non-negotiable for you.

Saying, "I hope I can do it" won't cut it. You need to state: "I'm going to become financially free in real estate by [insert date]. The amount I will reach is $[insert number], and I want it so that I will never have to worry about money again."

If you weren't born into privilege or means, it means you will need to build your mindset and resources from the ground up—but the advantage is that you'll want it more than others. You'll have the hunger you need to actually make it happen. When I started thinking that way, I also started seeing the challenges I faced as fuel. Even if there were some obstacles that slowed me down, I knew that I was still unstoppable.

As I started to see returns, my vision and passion for real estate deepened. From there, I saw that it was possible for all women to achieve the same results, so my vision broadened. I wanted to inspire other women who wanted what I had, and I started my company Wealth Building Concierge.

For you to become a wealthy woman with a Millionairess Mentality, you need to stay motivated and inspired. Right here, right now, I invite you to deepen your *why* as you start on this journey.

Money is Vital in Our World

Research shows that 54% of US consumers (125 million adults) are living paycheck to paycheck today, with 21% of that population struggling to pay their bills. This means they have little or no money left over after spending their income. Further, 68% of Americans will likely have very little or not enough to retire, and 50% of all Americans die with less than $10,000 in their accounts. They live on the edge of being destitute their entire lives.

If you're reading this book, you likely don't think that working long hours in a soul-sucking job for an over-bearing boss just to pay the bills is the life you signed up for. You don't want to have to work for decades to save enough to retire and finally start enjoying life. If so, you need to accept that money is a vital tool in our world and that anyone has access to it as a resource. Unless you're living deep in the Amazonian rainforest, money is a necessity. Making money can stress you out if you let it, or it can exhilarate you—driving your desire to get yourself a lot more of it.

Telling yourself that you don't really want or need money is the same as rejecting it. This way of thinking will repel money and keep you from achieving all that you're capable of. You will stay unmotivated and broke. Instead, you can start to value money as something that's good. Continue to focus on all the good that can come from it, for you and for others.

The truth is that it's just as easy to be wealthy as it is to struggle. Before I realized this truth and developed the Millionairess Mentality, I worked hard but not smart. Like most people, I made a good income by exchanging my time for money. There was no way to exponentially increase my wealth without another income stream.

If you are going to work, shouldn't you figure out how to make that effort as profitable as possible? This isn't about competing with colleagues for a position or leveraging yourself to take something away from someone else. No, you can earn more money by providing value through owning real estate and being well compensated for it.

Women Deserve More of the Real Estate Investing Pie

Approximately 93% of all millionaires are made from real estate, yet only 30% of all investors are women. Does it make sense that a majority of wealth from real estate is going to men? After all, in the past few decades, we as women have made great strides in our achievements. If that isn't impressive enough, we've also made babies and raised children who have become the leaders of this world.

There has been a shortage of solid education geared towards teaching women how to grow wealth through real estate investing and find the support they need. Women have been kept in the dark, believing that this type of investing is risky and complicated while men keep buying land and property. We want equal rights and to own more of the wealth, but to achieve that, we have to step up and take our seat at the table. No one is going to hand it to us.

I know failure is scary, but doing nothing is much worse. By reading this book, you're one step closer to closing the gap between men and women in this industry, so I hope you're getting fired up and ready to go. Prepare to roll up your sleeves and play to win—I give you permission.

Chapter 1 Actions:

In your journal or notebook, write out detailed answers to the following prompts. Committing these ideas to paper is the same as committing to yourself.

1. Declare your *why*: what is driving you to become financially independent and wealthy through real estate?

2. What does your financial life look like right now? Be sure to date this entry so you can track your progress.

3. Write out in detail what having money from real estate investing will give you. Be specific! This can be both material items (a beautiful home, college tuition for your children or travel) and emotional (the ability to give gifts without fear or to secure your own legacy). What do you

wish your financial life looked like? How will you feel once you get there?

4. State your goals: "I'm going to become financially free in real estate by _____. The number I will reach is $____, and I want it so I will never have to worry about money again."

5. What are you realizing about your ability to have money? (It is important to write your positive messages. The more you commit to them, the more your mindset will shift into abundance.)

TWO

WHY EVERY WOMAN SHOULD BUY REAL ESTATE

> *I will forever believe that buying a home is a great investment. Why? You can't live in a mutual fund.*
> —Oprah Winfrey

When I first started in real estate, even though my property was making so much money by appreciation (when the property itself goes up in value), it took me a while to believe I could actually retire on my investments.

Whenever I went to the "experts" (who were usually stock market guys who made a living on commissions from managing my money), they would tell me that real estate was risky. They would remind me I could get a bad tenant and get stuck making repairs. They told me I was calculating my returns incorrectly. And unfortunately, I believed them. I thought the so-called experts knew better than me and were trying to look out for my best interests. I mean, who was I to think I could figure out how to make money in real estate? I figured if it sounded too good to be true, which the industry certainly did, then I was either missing something or it wasn't for me.

But when I let the same "experts" manage my money, I didn't see the returns they promised, which made me feel like I didn't have control of my money. When I asked about diversification, they offered me annuities and bonds. I was at the mercy of other peoples' opinions and the stock market, and I felt helpless, like I could never reach my goals.

It wasn't until I did significant self-development work through therapy, the Landmark Forum and NLP to build up my self-confidence that I finally started taking some educated risks based on what I believed to be true. Then, finally, I took charge of own my portfolio.

Anyone (I Mean Anyone) Can Grow Wealth Through Real Estate

Real estate investors are often millionaires who struggled in school and never went to college. The reason for this is that it simply isn't that hard to understand, and you can make a ton of money from it. After all, land is a limited resource, and people always need a place to live. I'm not saying it's easy, and I've already told you it does involve risk. But it isn't *too* hard or *too* risky.

I have physician clients with the best education who say, "I can't wrap my head around real estate investing!" I always chuckle and say, "You can remove an appendix and fix a gunshot wound. Trust me, buying real estate is very easy by comparison." Ladies, it isn't brain surgery!

Once you know how to manage your finances and get a sense of how money grows through real estate, you'll feel much more comfortable stepping out of societal norms. This book is all about your ability to make different choices boldly—or at least build up your confidence about your choices.

Once you understand how to invest, you will never look back. You will see how many opportunities there are to make money and receive a stream of passive income every month. You'll no longer want to rely on disempowered ways of being. Of course, learning and getting good at anything takes practice. It may take you time to master investing, and you may also have some setbacks along the way. But you can't let those experiences discourage you. They will work for you if you're willing to trust yourself rather than the people who don't believe in your dreams. When you're mentally ready to become a real estate maven, you'll roll up your sleeves and be amazed at how much more money you can acquire.

If you can understand the process and the numbers, as well as talk to people and figure out where you want to buy, you'll have all you need.

Let's just take a quick look at the possible numbers. If

you put $50,000 into an investment that makes 8% annually, you'll earn $4,000 a year. That same $50,000 earning 8% a year will be worth $70,000 in five years; in 10 years, it'll be worth $90,000. In 20 years, your $50,000 investment will be worth $130,000—and this doesn't include compound interest or any additional investments you make during that time, so your real returns will be exponentially higher!

Following this model, you can do very little work to earn well over $100,000 (this is also calculating the interest on the $4,000 you earn every year)—plus, the value of your property will likely increase over time. You simply can't afford not to buy real estate if you want financial wealth.

But remember: nothing comes without consistent effort. Consistency isn't just a key for the wealthy. It's a time-tested truth that works for every person. If you start now, I guarantee you won't be in the same financial situation in 10 years.

Returns May Not Happen on Your Timeline, But They're Almost Guaranteed

The fact that you can't always time real estate returns by a specific date exactly makes people uneasy. Still, you can project numbers and possible strategies, and over time, almost every investment will be worth more than it is today. Yet, if an investment isn't worth the amount of money you're expecting in a certain timeframe or costs more to rehabilitate, you may think you made a mistake. Just bear in mind that most investment strategies will take time to mature—and in the following chapters, I will break down all of the options and variables.

There are so many things in life that we are powerless over, so we try to control what we can. Yet, the more we tighten the reins over those variables, the more we limit our results. For example, lots of people say they never want to lose money, so they have no option but to keep their funds in a bank account earning little to no interest. You aren't going to lose your money in front of your eyes, but with approximately 6% inflation (at this time of writing), you'll actually be losing 6% each year.

Inflation is the process where money becomes worth less as the years go by. It's a general increase in prices while the purchasing value of money falls.

In 10 years' time, you could lose 30% on your money as it sits in a bank account. Yes, $100,000 earning 0% interest over 10 years becomes $3,000 *less valuable* every year. Visualize it this way: imagine what a $100 bill is worth today versus what it was worth 20 years ago. Then, think of how the Dutch were able to purchase Manhattan in 1626 for $24 worth of beads and trinkets. Through these examples, you can start to understand how money compounds and the power of inflation.

Until I understood how much a few percent annually could add up, I let investment bankers make 2% or more a year on my hard-earned money regardless of what was happening with the stock market! I didn't want to tolerate that anymore, and my way out of that hamster wheel was real estate.

As it turns out, what you don't know *can* hurt you.

Real Estate Can Make You a Ton of Money Without Taking Over Your Life

One of the many things I love about real estate is that you can buy a property and make money without expending a lot of time. You can't use the excuse that you work a full-time job and need to take care of the kids. If you buy real estate correctly, tenants will pay you while you sit on the beach playing with your kids—no kidding!

I'm not talking about passive income from spammy Multi-Level Marketing (MLM) schemes or by selling timeshares. I'm talking about legitimate, hard assets that build generational wealth. While the real estate market can certainly fluctuate, prices will go up significantly almost without exception over time. I want to drive this point home. Can you tell?

Once you have money in the bank and are earning enough money to cover your living expenses, you can decide how to spend your time. You can make time to attend your kids' soccer games and dance recitals, and you can take vacations wherever and whenever you want. I'm not saying that you won't need to put in the work or that you'll never experience frustration, but given that you're likely going to work hard to earn a living anyway, this is a way to set yourself up for life.

Any excuses you can dream up can be dismissed because real estate deals are all *flexible*. Having no money, no skills, no team and no deals will not keep you from making real estate transactions, as you'll see once I break it all down for you.

Stop Playing Small

I once stood in a room of very high-achieving women who were all asked to share a win—and one after another, each of them downplayed their own greatness. They shared their achievements as if they were nothing when each one was actually a big deal. If this sounds familiar, you have likely overcome obstacles or achieved great things as well—but you've probably downplayed it.

When I was in my early 20s, I started to make good money and was acknowledged for my work in the entertainment industry. I chalked all my success up to luck. I also never knew how to take in that my achievements were taking me to great heights. I always compared myself to someone else—people who were further ahead than I was, both professionally and in terms of social status. It left me feeling bad about myself and negated all I'd accomplished.

As women, we never feel that we've arrived or will arrive. To fix that, we need to bust through the habit of playing and thinking small. This requires getting up every morning, rolling up our sleeves, getting to work and embracing our current greatness and potential.

Women need to own their own journey and feel entitled to their big dreams and visions. If we start owning that power, we can make huge shifts in our capacity to achieve even bigger things.

Our generation of women is paving the way for all women to grow in stature and make it commonplace to grow wealth. To join those ranks, the bottom line is that you need to decide you're smart enough and worthy enough. As my husband said to me the other day when I was working on a tough deal, "If it were easy, it wouldn't be worth doing."

Acknowledge all that you have accomplished so far and praise your victories. Respect yourself so that you can step into a larger version of yourself, because no one else can do it for you. You can either let your fearful thoughts limit and run your life, or you can step up.

If you're patient and follow the steps, there's no way you won't grow your wealth through real estate. If you can accept that your limiting stories are fiction and choose to let go of them, you can become who you want to be, creating the life of your dreams that's waiting in your heart.

Chapter 2 Actions:

1. Make a detailed list of all your accomplishments and achievements—and yes, this includes having kids, buying a home, maintaining a busy schedule and getting that last promotion!

2. Identify some of your self-limiting beliefs and areas where you "play it small."

3. Write out all the fears and fictions that you believe that are holding you back like this: "I can't ____ because ____."

4. What is one word that describes financial freedom for you? Abundance? Gratitude? Ease?

5. Now, write out what you *are* powerless over (such as the weather, for example). In a second column, write out if you can create a solution to move past that limitation. (Powerless: I don't have a down payment for a house. Solution: I can partner with a friend or family member who has more financial resources.)

THREE
KNOW YOUR FINANCES AND SET GOALS

66 *Every financial worry you want to banish and financial dream you want to achieve comes from taking tiny steps today that put you on a path toward your goals.*
—Suze Orman

Most women hear the word "finances" and want to run for the hills. They resent money for having power over them while at the same time letting it dominate their existence, living as victims to money stress as opposed to standing up and taking charge.

Learning to live in harmony with money isn't that hard, and growing wealth isn't impossible, either—but both things start with taking ownership of where you are right now, deciding where you want to be and moving in that direction. To that end, in this chapter, we'll go deeper into wealth-building strategies and how to protect your assets.

Right off the bat, I want you to know that I'm not a CPA, licensed financial advisor or attorney. Even so, I've made millions, saved hundreds of thousands in taxes and spent a lot of time learning from the best professionals—and my clients have also profited from my support. Now, I'm sharing my experience and proven methods with you.

However, I do recommend you explore any major financial decisions with a licensed professional. Make sure you educate yourself, too. CPAs and financial advisors don't know everything, and many don't understand real estate. As I mentioned, I got a lot of bad advice from so-called "experts" in my early days. As I taught myself and learned from the right people, my wealth and confidence grew in tandem.

If you aren't working with professionals who support your goals, look for a new team. Seek a lot of opinions and choose experts who share your vision and believe in you. Don't listen to your uncle who lost all of his money on one deal and thinks real estate is risky. Talk to people who understand—and have—what you want.

In my case, I instinctively knew I wanted to save as much of the money I earned as possible because it seemed like a great way to alleviate the stress of not having enough. I had no idea how to grow or manage money. If you're reading this book, you're light-years ahead of where I was when I started. Once you start loving your money and the opportunities you can create with it through real estate, you'll need to get the financial pieces in place to get everything moving in sync.

If You Don't Keep Track of Your Money, It Will Slip Out of Your Hands

You need to decide what system will work for you to track your money. Some women, for example, shouldn't use credit cards. They see something they like, and the credit card makes it easy for them to buy it, whether they can actually afford it or not. Remember: a dollar spent today could be worth substantially more tomorrow. Of course, there's no right or wrong way to track and spend; only what works for you as you move towards your goals. What's important is that you take charge over what you have and stay aware of the numbers.

You need to look at your finances at least once or twice a month so that you know what you have. That's the only way to manage and make money grow. There's a story of a UPS guy who only made $14,000 a year but who saved millions by the time he retired. There is no doubt that he was mindful of his spending and was an expert in his finances.

I was born without money, and I disciplined myself to buy only the things I could afford. Of course, I have still spent money on things that I scratch my head about in retrospect, but overall, I have stayed on track with my budget and stuck with it. I have always kept the bigger picture in mind of saving money and buying property so that while I was working my day job, my real estate was making money for me on the side. Once you get in the habit of saving money to invest, buying properties and seeing the profit, you'll feel incredible.

Write Down Your Numbers

It's proven that when you write down your numbers and goals, you're 60% more likely to reach them. Block out an hour each week of uninterrupted time to manage these tasks. The only one who's stopping you is you. It takes less time than you think, and once you learn how to track your expenses, you'll realize it isn't as hard as you thought. If you avoid keeping track of what you have and where you're going, the odds of success won't be in your favor.

Whatever you focus on expands, so if you're focused on money, you'll have more. This doesn't mean you are money-hungry! You're simply focusing on your goals. Having a system and budget for your spending enables you to create savings. This is the money you will likely invest, so you must become an expert in your spending habits.

The other thing you will notice is that when you start to track your money, you'll invite more money in. When you're not resisting money, you'll see the possibility of making more, expanding how much you have and how much you believe you can have.

It's also critical that you pay attention to how your investments are tracking. Growing your wealth in real estate requires you to move money around, so if you aren't tracking your finances, you can end up losing a lot. If you truly don't have the time to manage your investments, hire a bookkeeper—that's an investment that is a lot less expensive than the money you'd lose by ignoring your finances!

If your finances are simple, you don't need a fancy accounting program. You can use an Excel spreadsheet or simple bookkeeping software like Quicken or Google Sheets. You might even hire a bookkeeper to track a QuickBooks account for you and show you where you're spending more than necessary.

Always give yourself a deadline for checking your finances and log it in your calendar. If you don't do this already, it's a skill that will serve you well in real estate investing. You will become your own accountability partner.

It's also important to make sure you're saving a certain amount each month for unforeseen expenses. Real estate will almost always make you money, but you may sometimes be in the red for a few months. You need to be prepared for those times.

For even more structure than I provide in this chapter, you can take the Real Estate Investing Personality quiz and get the financial assessment masterclass based on the type of investing that works best for your lifestyle and circumstances at tamarquiz.com. Doing so will lift a huge weight off of your shoulders and will be a giant step toward buying your first (or second) investment property.

You might also consider joining my Millionairess Mentality Mastermind or another similar group for accountability. While you can also feel empowered by setting your own goals and deadlines, there's nothing like a hive of like-minded worker bees coming together to build a network of wealth through real estate investing! To find out more, visit my website at:

www.wealthbuildingconcierge.com

Either way, don't waste another second: put a monthly date in your calendar right now to track your finances.

Making Financial Choices and Priorities

There is a saying that financial guru Dave Ramsey says a lot: "If you will live like no one else, later you can *live* like no one else." When my clients start to look at their finances with me, they inevitably see places where they can cut back, save and make more money. Making small adjustments to your spending in order to save and then invest can make a huge difference in how the majority of your life will play out financially.

Look at your line items. For example, going out to

dinner three times a week will eat away at your potential savings fast. A lot of people throw their money at Starbucks every day—can you buy a tall instead of a venti? Get an Americano instead of a double-skinny-vanilla latte extra shot with whip?

Look at your utility bills: you may be able to lower your cable or cell phone payments if you call the companies and explore other plan options. A year ago, I switched my cable from one company to another and saved about $75 a month! It may feel like a lot of work to change your habits and small joys or to renegotiate with a customer service rep, but you'll have a sense of accomplishment and will get to enjoy all that extra money as you invest it later. If you really can't be bothered to spend a half an hour on the phone, have an assistant or a teenager looking for some extra cash make the calls for you. My kids have learned a ton making these sort of calls over the years.

I hope I don't upset too many of you by saying this, but buying new cars is a huge waste of money. I can't tell you how many times clients show me their expenses with a monthly lease payment of $600-$800 a month on a car! If you take that $600 a month and multiply it by 12, it equals $7,200. In five years, that's $36,000, which is enough to put a down payment on a property that could put you on the path to financial freedom.

I also can't tell you how many clients I have who spend way too much on rent instead of investing, saving or buying a home. They do this because they want to live in a certain area and don't want to modify their quality of life for the sake of getting ahead. Rent is the fastest way to blow your entire budget, and it leaves you with absolutely nothing to show for yourself once you move out.

I'm not saying to deprive yourself of nice things. For context, I've bought used luxury cars and have only purchased three new cars in my entire life. A few years ago, I bought a new Tesla, but I bought it when I could afford it and didn't have to take money out of my savings to do it. If I could not have afforded a new one, I would have been happy buying secondhand. Making these sorts of choices over the years has really made a difference in my bottom line.

Essentially, if you're spending more than you're making, it's very difficult to reach your goals. Though you will need to make some tough choices to avoid that, I'm not telling you to create struggle or hardship for yourself. Instead, find ways to make nice dinners at home and get a car you can enjoy, even if it's not a brand-new model—just buy a trustworthy used one so you don't throw away your savings on monthly expenses.

No matter what the specifics are, the simple rule is to limit the amount of money you have going out the door compared to how much you have coming in. Remember: with every nice purchase, you're trading luxury now for a lifetime of freedom later. If you can manage your finances correctly, you will be able to buy a brand-new car and the house of your dreams not too far in the future!

Think of this as a "money diet." If you start out with the goal of losing 30 pounds in a month and deprive yourself of every bite of food you enjoy, you'll get frustrated and quit—abandoning your goal all together. Be kind to yourself in the process of reaching your financial goals. Pat yourself on the back for small wins and structure your budget in a way you can *live* with. It's not about deprivation; it's about the long game. The most important goal is to save so that you can afford to start buying real estate and growing your portfolio.

Reassess Your Numbers and How You Look at Debt

Make a list of the good and bad debt in your life—and yes, there is such a thing as *good debt*. If you're borrowing money at a low interest rate to acquire a property, you get the benefit of leverage. This means you can put down 20% on a $500,000 property or $100,000 to get the benefits on a property valued at four times more. Of course, if you're using credit cards at 20% interest rates, you need to pay these off immediately and create a strategy for staying out of *bad debt*—or debt which depletes your assets and leaves you with no reward.

One exception to this rule is if you're using credit cards for a very quick turnaround deal, where you borrow as a bridge money loan. This means you're either providing a very short-term loan to someone, or you need the money yourself for just a few weeks. This sort of deal can be risky on a credit card unless you're sure the money will come in before your payment is due. Whatever you do, don't get stuck with a ridiculous interest rate. Do your research and protect yourself.

Take note of your list of current assets and where you can leverage them. One way is if you already own your house, which, let's say, has a $300,000 loan that's now worth a million dollars, you might consider taking out $250,000 in a cash-out refinance to buy a second property. Just be sure to check what the rates and fees would be on this type of transaction. If you haven't refinanced in a while, be sure to investigate the much lower interest rates that are available (at the time I'm writing this). Bear in mind that while you don't pay any tax on a refinance, your monthly payment will go up commensurate to your loan amount.

Another way to leverage your money through real estate investing is by using the money you have sitting in a 401(k). You can use it to earn interest that is tax deferred until you take the money out of the plan. I'll cover using your retirement plan to make money in real estate in the upcoming pages of this chapter.

Long-Term Strategy

One of the most challenging parts of wrapping your head around growing wealth is the ability to think long-term. You likely aren't going to make a million dollars overnight, so you need to create a plan and be consistent. I'll give you more details on strategy as you continue reading, but as an introduction, you must write out a vision of how much you think you need to live comfortably and how long you expect it to take you to reach your goal.

It's important to dream big and expand how much you think you can have. It may feel strange to say "I'm going to make a million dollars through real estate investing" when you're just starting, but carving out a visual picture of what that would look like for you will help you stick to your plan.

Ask yourself how you can have a nice life now while cutting back on some of the expenses eating away at your budget. Realize that you're investing in yourself and your future, and enjoy the idea that someday you'll be able to have so much more—including the things you avoid spending on now. Remember that you want to be able to live like most people can't; to do that, you need to do what's necessary to get there over time.

The more you can feel comfortable with letting your wealth grow, the greater wealth you will have. Getting rich quickly generally doesn't work, at least not for sustainable wealth. Case in point: 70% of lottery winners lose or spend all of their money in five years or less. So even if you were handed a million dollars, you would likely end up with the same amount or substantially less as the years went on unless you developed a strategy to grow it.

Figuring Out How Money Works

Often, my clients have hundreds of thousands in cash sitting in their bank accounts and are afraid to use it. They're fearful of making a bad investment or that the market will crash and leave them destitute. They're worried that they'll lose their jobs, their businesses will slow down or they'll need the excess money for some unexpected emergency.

They are often afraid to buy property because they're worried they might find something they like even better in a few months, so they end up doing nothing. They remain safe and frustrated, knowing that they will likely need to keep working just as hard as they are for the rest of their life without a break to keep up with their lifestyle. They assume they have no other choice.

Saving is good, but stockpiling money in your bank account is not growing wealth. Remember: the longer your money sits in a traditional bank earning 0.01%, the more its value decreases due to inflation.

If the frustration of knowing this doesn't motivate you, be aware that the banks take the money you park in your bank account and invest it for 8-20% returns! Wouldn't it make more sense to put that money in your own pocket? Opportunity cost is the money you're missing out on earning while you're thinking about it and sitting on the sidelines. The biggest risk of all is not investing your money.

You may be counting on the fact that your dollars are FDIC-insured—which means that should a bank go belly up, the US government will cover $250,000 per account. When you invest in stocks or any other commodity, that protection goes away. However, if you own real estate, you earn 7-25% annualized, and it can be just as secure as the FDIC-insured account. So it's a winning proposition to get your money into real estate.

The fears that keep you from acting will subside once you look at your finances logically. If you're nervous about having access to your money, put aside enough in cash reserves to cover your expenses for six to eight months. If you're worried about a medical emergency, spend a little extra money every month on a better health insurance policy. Get a life insurance policy. In other words, meet your worries with solutions.

Building Financial Security

In real estate investing, your objective is to make your money work for you in order to grow your wealth. To do this, you'll need to put your funds into buckets so that you're spending, saving and growing through tax advantages and investments.

To begin tracking your income and assets, download the free worksheet I've created at:

www.themillionairessmentality.com/assetbuilding

If you don't have any assets, you'll start building them with this book.

It doesn't matter where you're starting because every journey begins with the first step. But building assets should be your priority because they will give you money for a lifetime. A good example of this is the rent that tenants pay you.

All you need to start is two columns: one for what brings money in and one for what takes money out. Focus on bringing more money in than what goes out.

An **asset** is something that puts money in your pocket, as opposed to a liability that takes money out. An asset has value and can be used to meet debts. An example of a liability is a car that depreciates in value the second you drive it off the lot.

As your portfolio grows, you will need LLCs, trusts, insurance and more complex systems. These processes can be a bit confusing unless you think about them logically. I'll give you some bullet points on each topic for you to explore later in the following pages—just remember that I also felt blocked by my own growth and increased ability to invest at a larger capacity at the beginning!

I was stressed out by the responsibility of managing money. The things that saved me were knowing my numbers and trusting myself to piece out my priorities step by step. You will do the same. Don't worry and keep reading—I'm going to hold your hand through the whole process. We're going to break it down into simple, manageable steps and take them in order.

Committing to Your Financial Plan and Goals

What sort of life do you want to live? Figure out how much you *need* to live. If you cut it down to the bare bones, what would you require to cover your living expenses?

Next, figure out how much you *want* to live on. What's your dream number? If you could do everything—have that dream car, live where you want and travel wherever you want in the world—how much would you need?

Take some time right now to imagine all the things you want and put a price tag next to each item. If you're in the top tax bracket earning more than six figures, you need to add at least 30-40% for taxes. So, if you want $20,000 a month, you need $28,000 a month to be able to keep that

$20,000 for yourself. (There are ways to mitigate this tax burden, but you always need to assume you will owe the amount required by the government.)

Calculate the gap between where you are now and where you want to be.

You need to cultivate the Millionairess Mentality: *Everything that makes you money can help you multiply your wealth when you reinvest it.* Stay focused on the big picture and the long vision. Never spend more than you make and keep your *why* in mind to keep you motivated.

Using the Money in Your 401(k)

Most financial advisors don't tell you that your retirement funds can be self-directed. This means you can control what you invest it in, including real estate! Since advisors generally make no money on these items, there's no incentive for them to suggest it to you. Many of them are also not seasoned in real estate, so they aren't comfortable making those sorts of recommendations.

If you're working for a company as a W-2 earner, you often can't manage your retirement funds personally. If you leave a company and have 401(k) money from the company, you can take it out and make it self-directed. That said, you can sometimes take the money out before retirement age without paying the 10% penalty for a down payment on a first-time home or for medical emergencies. If you own a business, you can set up self-directed retirement plans without restrictions, although there are some parameters (depending upon whether you have employees and your personal objectives). This is an exciting option for real estate investors. You can also borrow that money (up to $50,000) and get loans, depending on how your plan is set up.

A traditional 401(k) plan is tax-deferred. You can't take the funds out without a 10% penalty until age 59-and-a-half. The balance will continue to grow, but at some point, you will owe taxes on money as you take it out of the plan.

With a Roth 401(k) plan, you can actually grow money tax-free. Though many companies offer Roth plans, they come with strict provisions. When you're making at least some multiple of six figures, you can use Defined Benefit plans and 401(k) plans to pay taxes and move money into a Roth account in larger sums. This is known as a backdoor Roth. (I wish I had used a Roth retirement plan sooner.)

This strategy is the same one that Peter Thiel, the founder of Paypal, used to turn $2000 in 1999 into a tax-free $5 *billion* in 2021. When investing in a Roth account, you use after-tax dollars to fund it and never pay tax on that money or any of its earnings again.

For the traditional Roth, at the time of this writing, if you earn $130,900 as a single person or $206,000 as a couple, you can add $6,000 to it per year (or $7,000 per year if you're over 50 years old). It isn't a huge contribution, but the nice thing is that you're using after-tax dollars, and as you have already learned, time is on your side! In 10 years, you will have added $60,000 to your account. If that makes 10% per year, that money will be worth double, tax-free.

The amount you can put into a retirement plan depends on the plan. Speak with your CPA or administrator for the self-directed 401(k) plan to confirm how much you can contribute.

If you have a lot of money and run your own company, you can set up a Defined Benefit Plan. By using an actuary to report your income to the government, you can put $100,000+ into those plans annually.

An alternative option with your 401(k) is to take the money out of it, pay the 10% penalty and use that money to buy a property. I've known people who have taken money out of their 401(k) because they don't like leaving their funds in plans overseen by the government. If you work for a great company, you may want to find out if they'll let you borrow money on your 401(k). You generally borrow up to $50,000 at a low interest rate and pay yourself back. Some companies have special incentives such as using your loan to buy a primary home, or for medical emergencies that enable you to withdraw early without incurring the 10% penalty (though both options will still result in taxes owed).

How Much Are You Paying in Taxes?

Don't underestimate the power of a good CPA or tax professional to support you in navigating taxes. Many seasoned professionals will give you different answers because the tax codes are complex and subject to interpretation.

You want to file your taxes by the book, yet still save money by understanding the tax code. There are a lot of incentives to save on taxes through real estate. Make sure to meet with your CPA quarterly, or at least semi-annually, and create a plan using the best tax advantages. Of course, make sure your CPA understands real estate.

How Much Are You Paying in Excessive Fees?

Traditional investing has trained people to save money and give it to an advisor to invest in stocks and mutual funds. You now know that many funds can be self-directed, and can be used to invest in real estate. If you use an advisor, be sure you also understand how much they are charging to manage your portfolio whether you're making profit or not. In addition, how much is the advisor making by selling you products like life insurance and annuities? (I do not recommend annuities! They're an extremely conservative way to invest your money, but they generally yield very low returns and lock in your funds for years. If you decide to buy one, make sure to read the fine print twice.)

The best thing you can do is educate yourself so that you understand the best opportunities available to you. Then you'll have a better sense of the best people to hire for your financial team.

Four Components to Ensure Financial Security

The following information could save you thousands. Don't skip over this list even if you aren't at a point yet where you have a large estate. I'm not going into a great amount of detail on these because there are tons of books available on these topics, but this is a good list to get you started—but read further about them on your own.

1. LLC

If you have properties that you're investing in, it's wise to protect those assets. Each entity, or at least a few of your properties, should be in an LLC (Limited Liability Corporation) together. (Talk to your CPA or attorney to see what they recommend.)

If the investments are in a retirement account, you don't need to put them in an LLC because retirement accounts are protected from lawsuits. But if you buy a single-family home and keep it in your name, you can be sued if someone is injured on the property. If that property exists in your personal name, all your personal assets and money are at risk, with the exception of your primary home. When you put the property in an LLC, all you can get sued for is the worth of that one property. Some CPAs believe it's overkill and a waste of money to have an LLC for each property because the likelihood of being sued for more than your insurance policy coverage isn't great, but it is still an option worth considering for peace of mind.

2. Life Insurance

Life insurance gets a bad rap. Overall, it is a great asset-protector, and the self-banking strategy through a whole life policy (when executed correctly) can be very beneficial in leveraging your money.

At the very least, consider a term policy, which simply states that for an annual premium, you're covered for a certain amount of money until a certain age. To make sure the proceeds of the policy go to the correct person upon death, designate your beneficiary.

If you're interested in maximizing the benefits of a life insurance policy, I work with a team that's the top in the country. If you're responsible for a spouse, aging parents or children, you want to make sure you have a plan in place. Feel free to reach out at hello@wealthbuilding-concierge.com for more information.

3. Living Trust

A living trust will allow you to designate all of your assets to your children or a designated party while avoiding probate. This trust gives you the right to elect a power of attorney to see that your wishes are taken care of if you're in an accident or on life support, and can also address any other wishes you may have regarding any minor children.

Probate is the process of approving the validity of a will.

A living trust also gives you a lot of flexibility to create detailed instructions for your assets (note that this is different from a will, which designates your wishes upon death only). These aren't pleasant topics to think about, but they are critical.

Without a living trust, your heirs might end up in dispute and litigation. I recommend finding an attorney to discuss the details with you. Don't skip this step! It makes no sense to create wealth if you won't be able to leave it to those you love after you're gone.

4. Medical Insurance

Today, there are many options for medical insurance, and while they can be costly, they're an essential expense to protect you and your loved ones. Since President Obama implemented the Affordable Care Act, Americans have been eligible to apply for insurance coverage once a year and can't be denied coverage for a preexisting condition.

At the very least, it's important to have catastrophic insurance for medical emergencies, as hospital treatments can clean out your finances quickly. If you have assets or savings and owe money to a hospital, they have the right to require you to sell everything other than your primary residence to pay off your debt. There's no point in buying a bunch of real estate if you aren't also protecting your health first.

I watched this very scenario play out with a family member, and it was devastating. My aunt had just one year left before qualifying for Medicare, so she cancelled her medical insurance policy at age 64. That year, she got very sick with cancer. The treatment was intense, and her lack of insurance made it so much harder on her family. Even after she lost her battle with cancer, the bills kept coming in and weren't easily forgiven.

My aunt owned property that she inherited, which was set up to support my uncle's retirement. During this whole ordeal, she considered selling it, but it was the only savings she had. I can't help but imagine how different things would have been if she had bought a few properties over the years—if she had, she could have sold one of them to pay off the hospital and care bills.

Chapter 3 Actions:

1. Do some research and interview CPAs and tax professionals. Have a list ready of what your financial goals are and find someone with the expertise to help you achieve them! Discuss Roth IRAs, your 401(k) and all other investing options aside from a basic savings account. Do they know about real estate investing? What are their fees?

2. Track your money. Find an app or a program that links to your bank accounts and portfolio so you can watch your money coming in and going out. Most money trackers will also categorize your spending, making it easy to see where the bulk of your money goes. Set up calendar reminders for you to review your money weekly, biweekly or monthly.

3. Make a list of all your *good* debt versus your *bad* debt (for example, *good* = a mortgage on an income-producing property, *bad* = credit card debt).

4. Write a list of every little corner you can cut to save some money. Coffee instead of a latté. Cooking an easy meal instead of delivery. Housekeeper once a month instead of weekly. Every penny and dollar counts! How much do you *need* to live? Now, determine how much you *want*.

5. Organize your money. Using these categories, make a chart: Monthly Cash Flow, Monthly Cash Draw, Paychecks, Bonuses, Savings, Emergency Cash, Monthly Living Expenses, Loans and Interest, Credit Cards and Interest, Properties Net Value, 401(k)/Retirement Plans, Stocks/Commodities/Bitcoin and Miscellaneous.

FOUR

YOUR REAL ESTATE INVESTING OPTIONS

> *My mom said to me, "One day you should settle down and marry a rich man." I said, "Mom, I am a rich man."*
> —Cher

There are so many ways to make money in real estate. If you're like most people, you probably think of it as buying and holding a property or as flipping houses. These are two great ways to invest, but there are others.

When I first started, I bought and held property. I was worried about losing money, so I did not use a ton of leverage (in other words, I didn't borrow a lot against my equity) or take a lot of chances. I still made a lot of money, but not nearly as much as I could have if I'd trusted myself and the numbers.

This chapter is designed to open your mind to new

ways that real estate can work for you. Remember: if an idea appeals to you, don't dismiss it by thinking it won't work. Always ask, "How can it be done?" This applies even if you think it's more than you can afford, or if you can't see exactly how the idea will be executed yet.

What's Your Real Estate Personality Type?

It's important to ask yourself what you think you'll enjoy about real estate investing. Do you think you'd love fixing houses and renting them out every month? Or do you want to buy a property and get a check every month without having to do any work? Some women love to get into the process and experience it all, while others are intimidated by repairs and chasing rent from unreliable tenants.

If you aren't sure yet what you'd like, jump in and find out! You will always learn and grow. This is a perfect time to pause and take my Real Estate Personality Quiz at tamarquiz.com.

The two distinct types of investors are known as *active* and *passive*. They're defined exactly as they sound. If you are active, you do a lot of work, and if you're passive, you do very little. The amount of money you have when you start investing will determine how passive or active you are.

In every deal, there's a money person and the person who puts in the "sweat equity." Sweat equity means you find the deal and do all of the required work—everything from researching the best kind of deal to attending open-houses and reviewing tenant applications. You may find that you want to be more involved with the rentals so that you can get certain tax advantages, charge management fees and justify some deductions with the government. This scenario typically works best if you have more time than money. If that's the case and you have the skills, you might even want to do some of the property repairs your-self. Sometimes, one woman can play all of the parts in the deal.

On the passive side, you may have a full-time career that prevents you from devoting much time to the process. Maybe you don't enjoy rolling up your sleeves or doing a lot of paperwork and you would rather have someone else do the heavy lifting. Perhaps you're further along in your investing career, have a substantial amount of savings and are ready to use real estate to multiply that money.

Some people do a combination of the two, but it's important to review all the strategies first. The clearer and more focused you are with your strategy, the better your results will be. Remember that there are three main factors involved in investing: money, time and the deal. We'll go over execution more in the following chapters. But for now, let's talk turkey: how do you get started?

Make Sure the Pieces Are in Place

If you're starting to feel overwhelmed or confused, that's normal. Don't worry—you'll learn as you continue reading and your progress unfolds. Before you go any further, please make sure that all of your action steps are completed and the financial pieces from the last few chapters are in order. Ensure that you have a balanced budget and a system in place to track your money. Be sure you have connected with your CPA, financial advisor and 401(k) administrator so that you know you're on track with all of your financial goals.

Ten Ways to Make Money in Real Estate

1. Buy and Hold

Buy-and-hold is a simple and solid concept. You purchase a property that is ideally growing in value (called appreciation) and giving you a return of income at the end of the month (called cash flow). In most cases, you're going to get more of one than the other, but it's possible to get both if you do your research and buy at a good price.

The property I purchased in 1999 is worth close to $1.5 million dollars today. I purchased it for $397,000. I can't think of another investment that grows this much almost guaranteed, and you don't need to do much but hold onto it.

My mom inherited $50,000 over 40 years ago. She then bought a property in North Hollywood, California for $65,000. Today, it's worth more than $650,000. She collects $2,900 a month in rent and has an asset worth $650,000 if she needs that money. She could certainly leverage that money to make more, which we will talk about in the next chapter, but a very simple buy-and-hold strategy also does very well.

Here's another way to look at the time and value equation. When you think about the price of an avocado 20 years ago, do you think it cost $2 per avocado? Probably not. Now, think of how much an avocado will cost 20 years from now. It's the same situation when you buy real estate.

You can get a 30-year fixed loan for up to four units that doesn't change rates for 30 years! In real estate, you're actually doubly taking advantage of the avocado concept because your property is going up in value while your interest rates *stays the same* for 30 years. This is a powerful concept. It isn't as exciting as buying Manhattan for $24, but it will still do wonders to grow your wealth.

A buy-and-hold option is a long-term play: you keep the property and earn solid monthly cash flow while you pay down the mortgage over time. If the property goes up in value substantially, you can also take out the profit in a "cash out refinance" or HELOC (Home Equity Line Of Credit for your primary residence) and use those proceeds to buy another property. Most of the time, one property won't be enough to enable you to retire, but over time, you'll accumulate properties so your cash flow and appreciation will add up.

2. Turnkey Operations

There are companies that offer what's known as turnkey operations, where you buy a property that's already fixed up with a tenant and property manager in place. All you have to do is collect the rent!

These companies are often involved in new builds or rehabbing distressed property that they then sell. Both of these opportunities offer sizable profits. Owners of these properties often have a broker's license, so that when the property sells, they get a commission for the transaction on top of the profit from the sale. However, because there's a long list of people to pay in turnkey operations, the seller won't receive as much cash flow or profit as an individual selling their own project.

If you're just starting out, working with a turnkey operator is a smart way to avoid some of the stress of finding a deal and making sure the numbers work. If it's your first go-around, don't worry about doing everything yourself or making the most amount of profit, especially if you're too nervous to take action. Investing in a turnkey property is infinitely better than not investing at all.

While you mitigate risk by investing in a turnkey, it's important to realize that even though the managers do vet the properties and place operators and tenants, it still isn't a risk-free transaction. At the end of the day, it's your property. If a tenant doesn't pay, the property manager will help you remove them, but it's still your problem. If an unprecedented event like COVID-19 happens, you'll need to figure out how to pay the mortgage if your tenants can't pay rent.

Also, even though professionals have already prepared the property in anticipation of selling, you should still hire your own inspector to look at the property. Run your own numbers, check references and look at all aspects of the deal.

3. Flipping

With this strategy, you buy a property at a discount because it needs repairs. You then rehabilitate it and sell it for a profit. This is one of the most common ways to make money in real estate. As most people have seen on popular TV shows, there's a lot of money to be made from this kind of investment, but there is also a lot of work and many variables that might create expensive speed bumps.

The truth is that flipping isn't actually real estate investing. It's more of a business that involves repairing houses and selling them. Even the IRS thinks of flipping in this way. Remember that your profit is only what's left after all of your expenses, *including taxes*.

Because the rehabs are typically completed in three to nine months, the profits are considered short-term capital gains. At the time of this writing, federal income tax rates range from 10-37% *of your income.* The savviest flippers take this into consideration and hold their properties for more than 12 months. After that, the properties are taxed for long-term capital gains brackets, ranging from 0-20%. Full-time flippers can be taxed at ordinary gains, which can be up to 37%.

All of that said, many people enjoy overseeing the transformation of a home and especially love the profits that come with the deals. In every real estate transaction, just be sure to stay aware of tax advantages and disadvantages.

4. BRRR (Buy, Rehabilitate, Refinance, Repeat)

This term was coined by Brandon Turner and David Greene of *Bigger Pockets.* First, you buy a property, repair it and get the profit out of it through a refinance. Then, instead of selling it as you would in a flip, you rent the property. You make your profit from the refinance (if you're working with a bank loan) so that you can invest it in the next property and repeat the process.

I like this strategy very much because it allows you to grow your portfolio, which is the key to long-lasting wealth. It also saves on the hefty taxes associated with flipping and rehabbing.

Of course, the amount of profit you make on a deal has a lot to do with the purchase price of the property. If you buy at a lower cost but the property is actually worth substantially more, you have built-in profit called "forced appreciation." Also, if you can get all of your down payment and rehab costs out of the deal in a refinance, you just purchased a property with a renter for no money out of pocket.

Forced Appreciation occurs when a real estate investor proactively increases cash flow and property value by raising the rent to market rate, adding amenities or property enhancements, or reduces expenses that will result in generating more income.

For example, let's say you buy a property for $200,000 but it's worth $350,000 ARV. You put 20% down for the loan from the $200,000 purchase price ($40,000), $30,000 for repairs and $30,000 for fees to refinance loans, equaling $100,000.

You subtract the $100,000 from $350,000, which leaves you with $250,000. You then pay back the $160,000 balance on the loan, get your $40,000 down payment returned and have $50,000 profit. Now, you have $90,000 for your next investment.

5. House Hacking

Buying a house and renting out the rooms is one of the best ways to start out in real estate. Rent is the most expensive line item in anyone's monthly expenses, so if you buy a property and live in it while getting your mortgage and expenses paid and avoiding rent, that's a pretty smooth deal.

Let's say your mortgage is $3,000 monthly and you can rent out four rooms at $1,000 each. This means you gross $4,000 each month with $1,000 profit. Of course, you need to be willing to deal with roommates and manage the money coming in and going out—it's all part of owning property!

Rent-by-the-room has become very popular, as you can find a large home and rent out each room like a hotel. The income from this strategy can be very profitable.

6. Airbnb™ and The Long Short

The short-term rental world has grown tremendously over the past 10 years. The core idea is that buying a property, furnishing it and renting it to others for a few nights or weeks at a time allows the owner to charge a premium. It can seem complicated to set up and manage, but most people who own these units are very happy with the extra income they bring in. It's more work up front, but once it's set up, most of the process is automated.

Many people buy a home and convert the garage into an ADU (Additional Dwelling Unit), renting that out for extra income. Be sure to check the local development and zoning restrictions, as some cities and neighborhood associations have strict laws and rules against ADUs and short-term rentals.

Airbnb and its counterparts—VRBO, Booking.com and others—were unstoppable until the COVID-19 virus hit in March 2020. When traveling stopped, so did all the business for Airbnb properties. Those who relied on the income from short-term rentals to pay their bills were unable to keep paying the expenses on their rental homes.

When investing, it's important to have reserve income stashed away in the event of slow months or national emergencies (pandemics and weather disasters are two examples). While it's a good idea to focus on mastering one strategy at a time, don't put your last dime into your investments. During the crisis of 2020 and 2021, I owned some Airbnb properties, but they were a small percentage of my portfolio. I was able to offset the loss from my Airbnb units with rent collected from tenants on buy-and-hold properties, so it's always a good idea to have a plan B.

I bought my Airbnbs in the Smoky Mountains, which are a one-hour drive from 60% of the US population. They have also long been a tourist destination with rental homes. For this reason, some people rented during the economic downturn because the area was easy to get to, and there are large enough homes there that a family can stay comfortably. The properties are also in Tennessee, which is a state that favors landlords rather than a state that favors tenants. You can check data, pricing and projections on AirDNA.com or data.rabbu.com.

If traveling nurses, executives or families relocating to a new state use your property for an extended stay (over 30 days), you can bypass the short-term rental fees or regulations in cities that prohibit short stays—and you can make almost as much money!

Long-term rentals have been a great strategy that my friend Julie Gates has coined "The Long Short," which refers to a furnished rental for more than 30 days. To learn more about short-term rentals, read *Short-Term Rental, Long-Term Wealth* by Avery Carl.

7. Syndications

Syndication is a completely passive investment strategy where a group of investors combine their money to buy large buildings such as storage units, multi-family dwellings, commercial units, industrial uses, mobile home parks or senior housing. This is a diverse strategy that can apply to any project that's too large or expensive for one person to finance alone and can involve making money on the back end in a few ways.

Syndications include two types of people: sponsors and investors. The sponsors are the people who bring in investors and are more active in managing the execution of a deal, whereas investors are the passive partners, giving their money to a sponsor they trust and letting them do the rest.

As with all real estate investing, there are no guarantees, but the profits on syndications tends to be excellent—anywhere from 7-20%.

Generally, syndication sponsors offer investors a preferred return paid monthly or quarterly, which is usually 7-9% annually on their money. You need to ask how soon preferred returns are expected to start being paid as the timeline can vary. As they enter a deal, investors also get an estimate for how long the deal will last before they can fully exit, which can be anywhere from two to 10 years. Upon exit, investors will participate in the share of the profits adding an approximate 7-10% annualized on the return to total 14-20% or more. You can sometimes invest in class A shares that pay a fixed 10% annualized return with no participation upon sale (for investors who prefer a steady return).

The strategy on many syndications is to take apartment units, buildings or senior residences and improve them so the property will appreciate and the owners can charge higher rents. The sponsors may also find a property for sale at a discount and get the "forced appreciation" I previously mentioned right out of the gate. The sponsor will generally sell once the property value has gone up substantially, ideally giving investors their projected returns and taking a portion of the profits for themselves.

For a property held for five years at a 20% annualized return, the overall return will be double whatever amount was put in!

If you think this sounds like an amazing investment, you're correct—especially considering most stock market returns average only 5-10% a year, and investors can do this strategy without putting in any of their own time.

Even though this may sound too good to be true, it's a very common type of real estate deal—but syndication deals are only as good as their sponsors. If you pursue this strategy, be sure to invest with someone who is experienced and knows how to calculate the numbers correctly. Look carefully at the summary they provide for the deal and understand how much they are charging in fees. As with any financial commitment or risk, you *can* lose on your investment. My company, Wealth Building Concierge, connects clients to syndicators and often has deals in the works as well.

Reach out to hello@wealthbuildingconcierge.com if you are interested in learning more.

8. Notes and Lending

Notes and lending are an opportunity for you to act like a bank. Essentially, you loan money to investors for their deals. This is an excellent way to make a great profit, again taking zero time from you other than monitoring the project. These sorts of loans usually pay 10-18%. A lender often charges points in addition to the annualized loan amount. Every point is equal to 1% of the purchase price. It's a similar concept as when you work with a mortgage lender.

What's the catch? You need to make sure you're lending to someone reputable whose project will be effective. A deal can go bad and lose you the returns you were promised, and even your initial investment. For this reason, vet the deal carefully. Of course, you can also get an attorney to write the paperwork for your protection. Make sure your name is listed as the first lien on the property so that if something doesn't go as planned, at least you can get the property back and sell or rehabilitate it yourself. Only send funds through escrow, never directly to the borrower—escrow acts as an intermediary to make sure all parties comply so that the exchange of funds is protected.

Many lenders also require that people put some "skin in the game," which means that they need to put at least 10-20% down. Sometimes they pay you the interest return monthly during the process of the loan. This adds another layer of protection for you, because if someone invests $20,000 in the deal, it shows they feel confident about the outcome.

As a private lender, you can make up your own terms or team up with a company that specializes in notes and lending. If you give your money to a company to lend on your behalf, you may get an 8-10% return as opposed to the higher opportunities mentioned, but this option mitigates your risk.

If the risks associated with the potential rewards above make you nervous, you might benefit from working with a mentor or coaching services like Wealth Building Concierge. Your risk increases when you aren't aware of all the variables or how to strategize around them. It can be very easy to lose money if you aren't working with experienced people you can trust, or if you don't know how to navigate the investment in the event it doesn't go as planned.

You can also work with fund managers who have lending groups that pay you a fixed premium of 8-11% annualized as long as you stay in the fund for a designated period.

9. Tenants in Common or Subdividing

As with all investments, you want to move with the changing times and manage deals that make sense. One of the biggest challenges in the world of real estate is how expensive it has become. As a result, many people start investing by having roommates like the house hacking method I mentioned above.

Along the same lines, in some larger cities, you can take a fourplex that would sell for a high price and divide it into four units—similar to a condo complex. This process is called "tenants in common." It tends to be a win-win for all parties, because it gives new buyers a way to get a smaller unit for a lower price; meanwhile, the owner can sell each of the four units as separate parcels, which enables them to get a premium on the sale.

Likewise, people are buying large homes and renting the rooms out to businesspeople or students in an area with a university. The idea also works with senior housing, where you create better accommodations for seniors at a premium price for the amenities.

If you are subdividing a multi-unit building, you need separate contracts and provisions for each of the four separate parcels of the fourplex. You need to work with the city to create these sub-parcels and make sure you're in legal compliance. Most of the regulations vary by state, city and county—though sometimes, the rules can even change from street to street!

10. Section 8—Low Income Housing

Section 8 low-income housing is government-subsidized. These are great opportunities to lock in rents at a regulated rate. During COVID, for example, Section 8 rents were unaffected. Tenants in these buildings tend to stay a long time, and the majority of rent is paid with a guarantee.

On the flip side, Section 8 housing can often carry more risk because the properties are often not in the best of neighborhoods. The cash flow on these properties is excellent, but the appreciation (how much they go up in value) is often relatively low. You need to check with the city to see if Section 8 housing is permitted in the area, or you can buy a property that already has established Section 8 tenants.

There Isn't One Right Answer

The Cheshire cat in Alice in Wonderland said it best: "If you don't know where you are going, any road will take you there." The hardest part of real estate investing is diving in, because you aren't certain whether to go left or right.

When you start out, there's a learning curve and a fear of the unknown. But just like a baby eventually learns how to walk—even if it means falling over again and again and collecting a few bruises along the way—so will you get the hang of these strategies.

The first step is to decide which option works for you. If you feel stuck because a few of these options could work in a few different states, just pick one and keep on moving. You're never going to get a 100% guarantee that everything will go your way with real estate, but isn't that true of just about everything? You can mitigate the risks, but you still have to get used to taking them. The alternative is not to try, and to watch others grow wealth while you stay in the same place.

Once I became comfortable with buying and holding,

I bought several more properties using that strategy. After a few years, I wanted to stop managing so many properties, so I invested in syndication deals and bought Airbnb properties. Real estate investing offers so many choices, and you can succeed with a little or a lot of money.

Focusing On One Strategy at a Time

I've already mentioned how important focus is, but this is probably one of the most important points I can make: a lack of focus is the reason people don't excel in anything! If you have too many things on your plate and too many ideas, it's difficult to accomplish even one deal—you get stuck in "analysis paralysis."

As I write this, I have to rein in my desire to go off and do 100 things at once. I've been guilty of talking to different partners about different deals and investigating dozens of opportunities, but not mastering one. I've taken the longer way around because I'm a person who likes variety. As a result, I've had to work a lot harder than someone who masters one type of investing at a time. When I started in this business, I bought duplexes in Los Angeles. I had a model that worked, so I repeated it until I discovered new ways to invest and felt ready to move on.

So beware of FOMO. Once you get going, there will be a fear of missing out on deals. Every project, city and investment may begin to sound as good as the next. Your friends will call you and tell you they just bought six properties in Kansas City while you were focusing on Tennessee, making you start to question whether you're in the wrong area. It takes time to build a team and a network in each location. Even if your friends have referrals, you still need to do your own due diligence. When you're just starting out, you don't want to have to build a new team every time you plan to buy a property.

Remember that there are lots of good properties and lots of good locations, so pick one concept and start in one place. Select what's easiest for you, and keep these ideas in mind:

- If you're a contractor or know about construction, you could do flips.
- If you're masterful at sales and know how to find deals and make them, become a wholesaler who mediates projects under contract with a seller, then offers them to a buyer for a fee (you'll learn more about that in the next chapter).
- If you're conservative and have time, do a buy-and-hold.
- If you are someone who loves design, you may want to pursue furnished rentals.

Note that even if you commit to a strategy, that doesn't mean you're going to put your money into a property right away. Still, by choosing an investment plan and taking action, you'll be moving forward and achieving your financial goals faster.

Chapter 4 Actions:

1. Determine your real estate personality—are you active or passive? List the aspects of ownership you are comfortable with. How well do you want to know your tenants? Do you want to review applications? Will you only flip and rehab? Are you handy? Do you have a team of contractors you trust at your disposal?

2. Research three different lenders and learn what you qualify for.

3. Pick your path! Plan to be nervous but move forward anyway. What outcome would you want out of that investment? What is your next move?

4. How much time do you have to reach your real estate goals?

5. Having decided whether you are an active or passive personality, how much time do you want to devote to your deals?

6. What scares you the most about investing? List some ideas to prevent your fears from coming true.

FIVE
EMBRACE INVESTMENT STRATEGIES

> *I always did something I was a little not ready to do. I think that's how you grow. When there's that moment of "Wow, I'm not really sure I can do this," and you push through those moments, that's when you have a breakthrough.*
> —*Marissa Mayer*

One factor that makes real estate more challenging than other types of investments is that there are a lot of other people who want to buy properties and a limited supply. Remember Mark Twain's famous words: "Buy land. They aren't making it anymore." Many people think they will strike it rich, so they have a cutthroat mentality. This is why it's important to maintain the belief that there's enough for everyone. One person can't get all of the good deals and leave you with nothing.

Nevertheless, finding a property can take a while, so you want to be ready to buy at any time. You also need to be patient and trust that your best investment is out there waiting for you. The good news is that regardless of how much you have saved or how comfortable you are with risk, there are options for you.

How Much Money Do You Have to Invest?

Once you've taken stock of your finances, you need to determine the amount you feel you can invest. That said, if you find a great real estate deal, it isn't hard to find other people who are willing to finance it for a piece of the action. If a bank loan isn't sufficient, you'll need to find other investors.

If you want to buy a property on your own, however, you must figure out a budget that can include paying realtors, closing costs, insurance, property taxes and repairs. Let's say you buy a property for $100,000 and can sell it for $100,000 without making a profit. You might pay a total of $6,000 in total closing costs plus the commissions to the realtors, which is usually anywhere from 2-3% for the buyer and the same for the seller. At 6% on $100,000, you're looking at an additional $6,000 to the realtors. So you have to make at least $106,000 on the sale just to break even. In a long-term hold, the property will appreciate, and you'll receive rent from tenants to help you reduce your mortgage. The profit can easily be well worth the investment, but it may not happen overnight—so make sure you don't need your money returned quickly.

If you're using a flip strategy, you can turn over profits quickly. It's great to get that quick cash injection, but remember that you'll owe more in taxes if you hold for less than a year. There are variables to analyze with each deal. Luckily, after you complete this book, you'll be ready.

Cash Flow and Appreciation

Cash flow is the amount of money you get as income every month after all expenses on the property have been paid—this is profit, and it's the name of the game! You don't need to work a job to pay your bills if enough money comes in monthly from rent payments.

Wealth-building is done more through appreciation, while cash flow gives you a monthly check. Bigger cities tend to provide more appreciation and less cash flow, but if you buy low enough, you can get both.

Cash flow in real estate equals the net balance of money left over each month after all expenses are paid on an investment.

Decide whether you're buying for appreciation, cash flow or both. Most successful investors pick one path to follow and are very specific about their objectives. If I want cash flow, I might buy 10 properties that will get me the most rent. Many people use Airbnb to make more monthly cash, which can be an extremely lucrative model (outside of the pandemic issue).

Another way to earn money in real estate is through forced appreciation, as I mentioned earlier. This means that you either buy a property under market value or buy a place and rehabilitate it to make it worth a lot more, having more control over its appreciation. Then, you rent it out.

If the area where you live is expensive and you can't afford to buy property there, go out of state. You may also be able to afford larger buildings in an area where the property values are lower. Imagine that 15 units could pay you $100-$400 profit per unit every month, netting you $1,500-$6,000 monthly. Of course, you would need to include the cost of a property manager in your budget!

How Much of a Return Do You Want?

You might be thinking, *I want the biggest return I can get!* But it's important to be realistic about the return you can get on your investment. If you're looking at a property in a popular market like Austin, Texas, you can be sure it's likely to appreciate, but it won't give you a lot of cash flow because of the high purchase prices. Some people are happy with a 5-7% return annualized while some want 10-12%. Deals with 10-12% returns often have more risk, but not necessarily. One of the things I love about real estate is that if you know the right people and how to find good deals, a 10-12% return on your investment isn't unreasonable at all.

If you want higher than 12%, you'll likely need to consider flipping, furnished rentals or partnering in a deal. It takes time to meet people, educate yourself and establish relationships, which is why a lot of new investors rely on coaches to get on a faster track.

One popular tactic in the real estate game is the 1% rule. If a property is purchased for $100,000, 1% is $1,000. If you can get a renter to pay $1,000 a month, you'll likely have some money left over after you pay your mortgage and monthly expenses—barring any larger unforeseen circumstances.

My expectations are high. I will shoot for 1% and want at least $500 a month cash flow *per unit*. If you buy a new property, you won't have to make as many repairs, which saves you time and money in the long run as long as you don't overpay up front. If you buy the property at a discount, it will be easier to hit that 1% on top of the built-in equity you'll have. In other words, if you buy a $100,000 property for 80% below market value and can still charge $1,000 per month in rent for, that 1% is suddenly more like 5%—that's a lot more cash in your pocket!

If you can manage not to lose money on your first deal, consider it a win. Most experienced investors will agree that the amount of value you get from experience outweighs breaking even or even losing a bit.

Where Will the Money Come From?

You'll need to figure out where the down payment will come from and how much of a loan you qualify for. This involves talking to lenders. Not all of them will give you the same information or rate, so make sure you speak to more than one and assess which ones will meet your needs and be easiest to work with. Additionally, lenders have different criteria, so one lender may loan to you while another won't. You can pull mortgage rates off the internet to help you choose which lenders to approach.

Getting a loan isn't difficult as long as you can show that you can afford to responsibly pay back the money. Before you talk to lenders, however, check your credit score with Equifax, Experian and TransUnion—the three main creditors—and make sure there are no errors on your credit reports, because they're more common than you'd think! The higher your credit score, the lower your interest rate will be.

I had a solid relationship with a lender who helped me out a lot when I needed pre-authorizations and a few loans. Then I had a duplex I wanted to refinance. I thought the rate was high and wanted a lower one. When I asked around and found a good lender, the one I'd worked with before told me to be cautious. I was warned that some lenders would change the numbers around at the last minute and wouldn't allow the loan to go through.

I still moved forward with the new lender, but I was nervous the entire time that they would cancel or modify the paperwork. At one point, my original lender told me my new lender couldn't actually give me the loan they were promising because the rates were already set by Fannie Mae and Freddie Mac. If they were to give me the rate they promised, the original lender argued, they would lose $25,000. Nevertheless, for whatever reason, I got the loan at the rate I was promised with no changes. Needless to say, I parted ways with the original lender after that.

The most important thing to remember when you're investing is that it's a business. You can't pay $10,000 extra because someone is a nice guy or gal. The numbers are what matters, and you're on a path to financial freedom. So, your goal is to get the best interest rate and terms possible and not to leave money on the table.

Expect a lot of paperwork. If you're buying a property with a conventional loan (this is a loan for properties with up to four residential units), the seller will ask you to submit a pre-approval letter from the lender to show that you can afford it. There are a lot of documents to fill out with loans, so make sure you read everything over and double-check that you understand it all before you sign. (We will break down different types of loans further in

Chapter 6.) If you're buying five or more units or a commercial building, the lender will look at the amount of profit the property will generate and assess the cap rate, not your personal income.

Of course, if you have the cash, you can buy the property without a loan and avoid the pre-approval process. If you pay all cash, you aren't taking advantage of leveraging money, however, so I generally like to use as little cash as I can and borrow the rest at a low interest rate. You can borrow the money from a hard money private lender, a person who loans money at a higher rate but offers it with a quick turnaround. If you go this route, refinance eventually into a conventional loan. You can also use DSCR loans (Debt Service Coverage Ratio) which are based on the rental income and not your income. Again, less paperwork!

As I mentioned before, you can also buy the property through a 401(k). I was taught that this was a great idea, so my husband and I socked away a ton of money in retirement and paid for our properties in full through our plans. We could never take advantage of depreciation, but our accounts were growing in profit.

Once we take money out of our 401(k)s at retirement age, those distributions will be taxed. Consult with a few CPAs about your plan before you go this route. Most of them will advise you to continue putting your money in your retirement account so that it can grow tax-deferred. This is the traditional idea which the government set up with many tax incentives. Some people like to use real estate outside of the plan and don't like the limits on tax-deferred strategies, but I want you to know all of the options.

Clients often ask me where to find a good lender. Getting recommendations from people you trust is a good place to start. Still, even when you get a referral, that doesn't necessarily mean that person will work for you.

At one point, I was looking for a financial advisor. I got a referral from some people I knew who had a lot of money and seemed to know what they were doing, but the advisor ended up selling me a bunch of annuities. I don't think annuities are the worst things in the world, but most of the products he sold me lined his pocketbook more than mine. He tapped into my fears about losing money in the stock market and real estate.

Annuities generally don't earn more than 3-7%, and they are long holds with steep penalties for taking money out early. My real estate deals all earn over 10% plus tax advantages, yet the expert told me real estate investing is risky. Later, I asked my friends about this so-called expert. They admitted they'd used him for specific things and hadn't bought any of his products. I should have asked them about it beforehand.

The bottom line is that you always have to vet your recommendations carefully. Also, if something doesn't sit right with you or you can't understand how an investment works, it's probably not for you. Trust that feeling. Even though I lost a lot of money getting out of those deals and my opportunity cost (all the time my investments sat there making no money) was great, I learned so much from that experience. It made me a better investor!

As I've said, the advantage of borrowing money is the leverage component. If you put 20% down on a $100,000 property, you have $20,000 invested. The property is worth $100,000, and the bank is allowing you to borrow the money for the rest. If you earn $300 net per month in rent, you make $3,600 annually, which is 18% on your down payment. Plus, you own an asset valued at $100,000! In other words, the money you're borrowing to buy the whole asset only costs you 4-5% interest, but as you pay it back, you're still able to make money on the *entire* asset.

You can also make your 401(k) funds self-directed and explore using FHA loans, second home rates and rates for less than 30 years if you know you won't be holding onto a property for more than five to seven years.

How Much Do You Want to Put Down? (OPM— aka, Other People's Money)

Contrary to the way most of us understand money, the bank isn't the only entity that lends it. There are private lenders—as well as friends, family and partners. I think a whole book could be written about why borrowing money from friends and family isn't a great idea; it's just not the first place I would look for funding. But if you're on the younger side and need help with a down payment for a house, a parent can be a very reasonable person to ask.

When borrowing money from people rather than the bank, there's no difference in how the legal documents are written— there's still a promissory note and a lien on the property if someone defaults. Still, you also usually pay a premium in interest on these loans (called "hard money loans"). Flippers often use hard money loans for their properties because a bank generally won't allow borrowing on a house that's in poor condition.

The hard money lenders know flippers need the money, so they charge upwards of 12% plus three points (remember that each point is equal to 1% of the purchase price). It may sound like an outrageous amount of money, but the lenders are taking a substantial amount of risk if something goes wrong with the property. Also, flippers stand to make a substantial profit on the deal if they can borrow the necessary money for purchasing. If you have the time to manage the property and find a great deal, you can usually find a lender to loan you the money.

One of the best ways women can get started in real estate is through partnerships. Start looking for a partner by talking to people you know and meet. These days, it's a lot easier to find partners because of the social networks we have available to us. There are meetups, podcasts and events that all enable you to meet people who can help you move forward with your investing goals.

The seller can also finance your loan, which is known as "seller financing." If there's a lot of equity in the property, a sale can trigger a large tax event that the seller may want to avoid, so they finance the property to the buyer. You can negotiate whatever terms you want as long as both parties agree. Often, the seller may need some cash, so they'll agree to a reasonable monthly payment and interest. The seller also holds first position on the note on the property, so if you default, they can get their property back.

Location, Location, Location

Location has always been one of the most important factors in real estate, and it always will be. Clients often ask me, "Where's the best place to invest?" The truth is that there isn't one best place. The best is the one that fits all of your individual criteria and where you have people who can support you if you're out-of-state. But choose a state or city that's more favorable to landlords because the state will then protect your rights as the owner.

You might want to look for a city or neighborhood you are familiar with or where you have partners or family. While Los Angeles is a very expensive market, I grew up here and have seen firsthand how property values have increased over the years. I know the number of jobs available here, and I understand both the metropolitan market and the shortage of housing. For these reasons, I'm comfortable making deals in LA. Also, because I know people and have partners in projects in Southern California, I don't need to buy all of the properties myself. While I don't make all of the profit, I minimize my risk if anything goes wrong.

Find out the answers to these questions about any area you're considering:

1. Is the area desirable for people looking for a place to live?
2. Is the city putting money into the area with construction and new businesses?
3. Are other people fixing up places?
4. What are properties selling for?
5. Are there jobs available in the area?
6. Are there restaurants and other businesses around such as Starbucks and Costco?
7. Are properties in the area appreciating?
8. Check other properties to see if the real estate has gone up in value over time. (Property values can be very different even from one block to the next, so check carefully.)

Real estate investing isn't rocket science, but you do need to be thorough. Don't rely a friend of a friend or even a good friend for reliable information. Even if the potential purchase is outside of your area, you must:

1. Visit the property yourself and do your best to see the interior.
2. Only trust people who are working for you and have your best interest in mind to visit and investigate the property in your place. You can find realtors, property managers, construction crews and investment partners who will work for your best interest. Nurture those relationships!
3. Talk to the property managers about properties you're interested in (they can make or break your deal).
4. Talk to neighbors about the area.
5. Stand in the backyard and see if there's a lot of noise.
6. See if there are other properties being rehabilitated in the area. If there are, this is a great sign because it shows gentrification, which means others are investing there. (Gentrification can be a hot-button issue, so consider the local sociopolitical climate and how it might lead to changes in local tenant laws.)
7. Visit local stores to make sure you like what you see.
8. Drive by the place at night. Do it twice!
9. Get a professional inspection.

While some areas are inexpensive and will yield a decent cash flow, they can also be risky investments. It can be difficult to determine how many people are living in the area, and these homes often don't appreciate well. However, if you're buying solely for the cash flow and can get 1-2% on rents proportionate to the purchase price, you can take home quite a bit of money. But do your due diligence first!

Sometimes, an area will change over a period of years from undesirable to a multimillion-dollar location. This has happened in so many neighborhoods in Los Angeles like Venice, Culver City and Echo Park. Years ago, these were dangerous and dirty parts of town. Twenty years later, few can afford to live in them. Imagine if you had picked up a few of those properties!

For areas that have become very popular, it's a great idea to look at neighboring towns. Those areas may not yet have gentrified, which makes them a great investment opportunity as the gentrified area expands into those surrounding towns and neighborhoods.

When won't a property appreciate? If you live in an area with one main industry for workers or a low population, you may never get a higher demand on the price. If you look at Detroit during the era when the car industry was wiped out and the state economy was decimated, you can see how this scenario can play out.

Market Timing: Spring Versus Summer

When you buy your property is also important, because more buyers are out looking during certain months. For example, December isn't a great month to rent or sell a property, as people are busy with the holidays and year-end tasks.

Recently, I bought a newly constructed single-family home that closed in November. Unfortunately, no one wanted to rent between Thanksgiving and Christmas, so I had to wait until February to find a tenant.

I could have purchased in a more populated area or hired a realtor with a better handle on the market. If I had, I would have known that it wasn't the best time to find a tenant. In other words, do thorough research and hire better support. That said, sometimes you need to be patient to find the right tenant if the buying time isn't perfect.

Of course, no one can predict the market entirely or know when a downward cycle is coming. The best thing you can do is to analyze and reanalyze what's happening at the time and speculate on what you believe will happen in the economy and your particular market. If you're dead set on buying a property before the end of the year, one to two months won't break the bank on a great deal. If you find someone who suddenly must move and is selling at a discount, the numbers may make sense to just go for it!

Finding Your Deal

Your investment opportunities will depend on what deals you have access to, who you know and the volatility of the real estate market. It can be overwhelming to determine where to look for a property, so I suggest breaking this daunting task down into steps:

1. Decide how much money you have to invest.
If you're on a tight budget, for example, you won't be able to afford to invest in Los Angeles unless you have partners. In that case, you'll want to look at places with more affordable properties. Spend some time on Google looking at property values and listen to podcasts that discuss good places to invest. Check out biggerpockets.com, which offers advice on real estate investment locations. If you don't need cash flow right away from tenants, you have more flexibility to look at long-term holds where the value will appreciate more.

2. Narrow down your options to two or three properties that you want to explore further.
Then, research each as we discussed in the Location section and talk to other investors in the area. Visit the properties if at all possible. Definitely don't just take the advice of the person who primarily wants to sell to you.

3. If you want to borrow money, talk to several lenders. Bear in mind that you can't just walk into a bank and ask for $500,000. When your property contains fewer than four units, they will evaluate the loan based on comparable properties in the area (also known as "comps"). This shows them the value of the property, how much money you can make and how much you can afford to pay. If you're buying a building with more than five units, the lender will look at the cap rate of the property and how much they think you can collect in rent every month. Larger loans are more complicated, so I don't go into great detail about them in this book. After all, most investors don't start out buying a multi-family building. Since these larger units tend to be expensive, many people take on partners to purchase them. This way, you don't need to come up with all of the money by yourself.

A **cap rate** means "capitalization rate," which refers to the ratio between the annual rental income from a property and its market value.

4. Should you buy at market value? If you plan to hold the property for a while, expect it to appreciate and believe it will bring you monthly cash flow from tenants, you don't necessarily have to get a deal for 10-20% below market value in order to see a profit. If you're eager to find a discount, however, you could find a distressed property, which means a building that has been abandoned and is in need of repairs. These often have overgrown bushes, a deteriorating exterior and perhaps even boarded-up windows. You can find these deals by doing something called "driving for dollars." In this case, you pick areas to drive through looking for such buildings. Finding the owners of properties like these is called "skip tracing." You can find the addresses of owners in public records with the city or through apps. For any distressed properties you're interested in, call the owners and send them letters. Be sure to set up a website that says "We buy homes" so that they see you as legitimate. And of course, list your website address in the letter you send them.

Hiring a Realtor

Hiring a realtor gets its own section because it's *so* important! Let's look at selling and buying scenarios. If you decide to sell a property that you own, having a good realtor can make or break your deal. They are expert representatives on your behalf, making sure you have a smooth transaction. As seller's agents, they ensure you get the best price.

Even if your best friend highly recommends you realtors, make sure that you check their references and vet them yourself. I made the mistake once of taking a recommendation without properly vetting the agent, and it cost me time, money and aggravation. I signed an agreement committing to that realtor for six months with no out clause, and she didn't want to let me out of my contract even though she wasn't finding a buyer for me. So, whenever you sign an exclusive agreement with a realtor to sell a property for you, always include a clause that allows you to get out of the agreement (minus any expenses they incurred) if you aren't happy with them.

This is a good time to remind you not to sign anything you don't understand or that doesn't sit right with you. Get an attorney to vet agreements because real estate forms are binding. In my case, I was eventually able to break the agreement and move on, but it was more of a headache than it needed to be. *Always read your contracts!*

If you're looking to *buy* a property, there's no reason you have to work with a realtor at all. Nevertheless, realtors often have access to deals, know the best areas to buy and know the price potential for appreciation in their region. Realtors who are also investors can help you find different opportunities that can lead to profit and cash flow. As buyer's agents, they check that buyers are abiding the law by disclosing any repairs or problems with the property.

When you buy a property, the seller is responsible for paying all realtor fees. For this reason, there are times when the seller may be willing to sell to you without a realtor, which saves them the fees—a savings they may be happy to pass on to you in a discount on your purchase price. If you go this route, however, you need to make sure to get an attorney to help with the sale. A lawyer will usually set up an escrow account to transfer all of the funds between the parties and make sure there are no outstanding liens on the property. You may save money if you do it alone, but you also lose some of the security of having a team to protect you from potential problems. Another idea is to obtain your own real estate license or find a realtor who will reduce their commission if they don't have as many responsibilities to orchestrate in the deal.

> A **lien** is the right to keep possession of property belonging to another person until a debt owed by that person is resolved.

Auctions and Probates

One of the best ways to make money in real estate is to

purchase properties at a discount through auctions and probates. An auction often includes properties that are being sold at a discount because the owner is in distress or someone wants to turn over the property quickly. You can find out about these on auctions.com by attending either live or online. You usually need to pay for these properties with cash, however, which is one of the reasons they're sold below market rate. Check that there are no liens on the property, because if you buy without checking, the original owner's debt could be transferred to you as the new owner.

Another potential problem with purchasing through an auction is that you are sometimes restricted from looking inside a property. If you can't run an inspection or view the interior, there are a lot of unknown variables that could prove problematic. Many people who buy properties at auctions buy several buildings at a time, which enables them to lose on one and still make a profit on the others. It may sound crazy, but the under-market value on these can be huge.

You can also get discounts on properties through probates. This is similar to an auction in that you often can't see inside the property, and you must pay with cash. If you don't have the cash, you can find a lender and use hard money rather than a mortgage. Probates occur when a person who owns a property dies without having designated who should have rights to ownership after their passing. In this case, when no one claims the property, the court sells it to bidders. While these properties are usually sold under market value, the bids can skyrocket quickly. I once observed a property go up in bids from $2 million to $4 million in five minutes!

Foreclosures and Short Sales

There are more opportunities to pick up properties at a discount with foreclosures and short sales. These occur when an owner defaults on the home and can no longer make payments.

Both of these situations can be transferred to auction houses or dealt with by a bank. The bank generally doesn't want a property sitting on the books making no money, so they'll offer the deal at a discount to sell it fast.

With a short sale, the realtor can negotiate with the bank to sell it at a certain price below market. Then the bank needs to agree to relieve the property for the lesser price, which can be a lengthy process. It can be a bit of a hassle and requires patience.

You can sometimes get one of these properties by establishing close ties with a bank or by attending an auction on the courthouse steps. Again, you need to come with cash.

While there is so much more to share about foreclosures, it's beyond the scope of this book to discuss it in detail. I want to simply give you an introduction to the concepts so that you can dive into the strategy that excites you most. If this strategy interests you, there are many resources to help you explore it further. To learn more about buying foreclosed properties, read *Bidding to Buy: A Step-by-Step Guide to Investing In Real Estate Foreclosures* by David Osborn and Aaron Amuchastegui.

Wholesale

Wholesale offers another opportunity to invest at a discount. A wholesaler is essentially a middle person between the buyer and seller who scrounges for discounted properties so that the buyer doesn't have to. They find distressed (or otherwise highly motivated) homeowners and agree to put their houses under contract to help them find a buyer quickly. They usually get anywhere from $5,000-$30,000 *plus* (depending on the deal and the size of the property) for finding the buyer and handing over the contract. If the price is right, the wholesaler makes a profit, and so does the buyer.

Wholesalers make it their business to get the deal first and then pass off the discount to the potential buyer or flipper. The top wholesalers can make a substantial amount of money as they build a reputation for finding properties and moving deals. Of course, in these situations you have less security than when buying through a real estate broker because you aren't conducting the customary inspections. For this reason, you might find that some of the properties have some problems.

A broker is a real estate agent who has completed additional training and licensing who acts as a liaison between the buyer and seller, or property owner and renter.

Still, if you can get a deal at a steep enough discount, the potential profit can be enough to allow you to pay for any issues. Wholesalers will automatically tell you that a property will only cost a certain amount for repairs but remember that their estimate is no guarantee. Since they're known for telling buyers what they want to hear in order to make the sale, enter into these partnerships with caution—even if they can be a great way to acquire properties.

Syndications: Passive Investing

As you'll recall from Chapter 4, syndications are passive investments, which means you do no work. You can invest in syndications from your personal account or from a self-directed 401(k) that supports the strategy in the document terms. If you use a 401(k), you don't get the tax deduction, but you do get to grow that money tax-deferred. Be sure to check with your CPA to see if you would be subject to an UBIT (Unrelated Business Income Tax) for leveraging your retirement funds.

These calculations are much more intricate than when you are just investing in a one-to-four-unit property. Look for a cash-on-cash, 7-9% annualized return received quarterly or annually and an exit projection of a total 15-20% annualized return. Based on these projected numbers, you can count on doubling your invested funds every five years ($100,000 x 20% for five years equals $200,000). If I project a return that's 20% annualized, it's a deal worth pursuing.

Recently, I invested in a 180-apartment complex in San Diego, California. The sponsors sold it because with COVID-19, the restrictions made it challenging to scale. After three years, I still earned 10% annualized, which wasn't bad for a worst-case scenario. Remember that the sponsor's experience and confidence in the deal are key. You will not have any say in the management of the investment most of the time, so ask all your questions before investing. For help with questions to ask a sponsor, go to:

www.themillionairessmentality.com/vetsponsors

Use a Checklist to Pay Attention to the Details

Create a checklist of all of the questions you might need to ask yourself about a property so that you don't forget anything important. Here are the main questions I suggest, but for a complete checklist, visit my website at:

themillionairessmentality.com/questionstoask

1. Is the asking price versus the amount of rent I would earn a good value?
2. What price would make this property a good deal?
3. Did I do an inspection?
4. Do I have a construction crew in this area?
5. Do I have a property manager in this area?
6. Have I visited the location and driven around to see if I like the area?
7. Do I think the property will likely increase in value over time?
8. If I purchase this property, can I comfortably keep a bit of savings in the event I need to do unforeseen repairs or a tenant moves out?
9. Can I afford to hold this property for at least three years to ensure I don't lose money?
10. Do I have a realtor that understands investments and is looking for the best properties for me?
11. What is stopping me from saying yes to a property and putting in an offer?

Pick a Strategy and Do It!

I love how Brandon Turner of *Bigger Pockets* focuses on mobile homes. When he was asked if he thought mobile homes were the absolute best investment, he said they weren't—he got into them because he needed to pick one thing, so he decided to get really good at them so that he could maximize his profits through just one strategy.

As Brandon's story shows, strategy enables you to get good at one thing and stay on track. You can do the same. Focus, and put a plan in place before moving full steam ahead. Once you master that strategy, you can try another one. Remember that owning real estate and building wealth through assets is a matter of determination and action steps.

A critical factor that will determine your success is your knowledge and understanding of the numbers. That's what you're going to learn next!

Chapter 5 Actions:

1. Determine how much you are able to invest.

2. Decide whether you're buying for appreciation, cash flow or both.

3. What are your return expectations on your potential investment? Select three properties that interest you and compare the numbers.

4. Check your credit score at the major credit companies and then research your loan opportunities.

5. Thoroughly research the city, neighborhood and neigh-boring towns. Pay attention to comps, appreciation, local industry, the job market and local development. Write down your target investing location (city, neighborhood and so on).

6. Hire a realtor! Visit the area, go to networking groups, meet wholesalers and become a local expert.

SIX

UNDERSTAND THE REAL ESTATE NUMBERS

" *Enthusiasm is common. Endurance is rare.*
—*Angela Duckworth*

Do you have math anxiety? I'll bet you're better at it than you think. In an article published in *Scientific American,* Colleen Ganley observed:

> Girls tend to have less positive math attitudes:
> They have higher levels of math anxiety and lower
> levels of confidence in their math skills. This
> means even when girls show similar performance
> levels to boys, they are often less sure of
> themselves.

These doubts tend to hide under the surface, so women often don't realize they've been socially conditioned to believe that they can't understand certain concepts. Imagine letting the inaccurate belief that you can't properly evaluate numbers stand between you and growing your wealth in real estate!

It's true that numbers are very important in real estate, and they may be complicated at first. Still, with a little practice, they aren't difficult to understand. You have to understand cap rates and cash flow and be able to do a few calculations, but for the most part, everything makes logical sense.

On a very basic level, the profit on a property equals the income from tenants minus your expenses. How much did you bring in and how much money did you spend? If the amount that you brought in is greater, you made money. If you bought a property for $100,000 and can sell it today for $140,000, take away the $10,000 fees for realtors and closing costs, and you made $30,000. For the most part, it's that simple.

In the beginning, I also needed spreadsheets explained to me, but with some practice, I could understand them. Now, reading them is second nature. I'm sure that's true for you as well. Had I not followed my goal to reach financial independence, I may never have pushed through my math anxiety barrier. I would still be working in a profession that didn't feed my heart. I would still need to get up every morning and put in my eight hours at a company.

Today, I'm not afraid of the numbers. I analyze them thoughtfully and know I can trust myself. If the numbers tell me I can make what I want or close to it, I'm confident. If I'm ever not sure, I have friends with a lot of real estate experience who can offer me their opinions.

You can set up a spreadsheet or use the calculators on the Bigger Pockets website to figure out your own math. You simply need to be aware of all the potential expenses so that you can calculate accurately. For example, if your building is old or hasn't been maintained, you may have to make repairs (when a property has been neglected, we say it has "deferred maintenance"). In those cases, you'll need an inspection as soon as possible so a professional can help you understand how you'll need to budget your expenses. Over time, however, you'll even be able to predict some of these surprise expenses.

When people get confused about real estate, it often has to do with the calculations used to analyze deals. But here's an insider secret: you can use a variety of methods to track your numbers. There's more than one way to calculate. If you're still doubting your math or results, ask a friend with experience, join a mastermind or find a realtor to support you with the process.

I'll confess: I'm pretty good at math, but I've had to study some of the real estate equations several times to fully understand them. If you're brand new to real estate, you can't beat yourself up for not being able to comprehend everything right away. Whether you use Excel, an app or pen and paper, you'll get the same results as long as you're accurate about the income and expenses.

Be kind to yourself and know that there's a learning curve that you, too, will eventually master. Now, let's get started.

How Real Estate Makes You Wealthy Over Time

With real estate, after factoring in appreciation, paying down debt on a loan, monthly cash flow and tax incentives, it's very common to earn over 12% on an annualized basis. Compare that to 0.05% annualized from money sitting in the bank or an approximate 7% annualized from the stock market, and it becomes clear how powerful real estate investments can be.

If you have $50,000, you can use $40,000 for a down payment on a $200,000 home and borrow $160,000 from the bank. You then have $10,000 for closing and for repairs and vacancy. The funds for repair and vacancy are a cushion fund, and they are critical protection for all investors in case something goes wrong with a property, the tenant moves out or there's a roof leak.

Your income is generated based on the amount you receive from rents. All of the income that's generated after expenses is cash flow. Let's say the purchase price was $200,000, and you put down 20% or $40,000. Let's say you're getting $2,000 a month in rent. After expenses, mortgage insurance and property tax, you estimate you will have $250 left.

For this hypothetical situation, with a monthly cash flow of $250, your annual income would be $250 x 12, which is $3,000 a year (barring any unexpected expenses for repairs or vacancy). You could save that money, spend it or pay more down on the principal loan. Most investors don't necessarily pay down their loans because the interest rates are so low (currently at 3-4%), so it makes much more sense to reinvest the money and gain 10-12%. If you want a very simple life, you can pay down your loan completely. Once you pay off the mortgage, all the cash flow plus what you were paying toward the loan will go in your pocket. It will increase your cash flow, but it won't exponentially move the needle on your net worth.

While $3,000 a year isn't enough to retire, that amount can still multiply quite quickly. If you add 10 properties that each make $3,000 a year, that's $30,000. If the property goes up in value 3% a year, you earn appreciation on the home beyond your $40,000 initial down payment. You can't necessarily count on appreciation, but in most cases, depending on the property location, you can assume that whatever your property is valued today will increase exponentially in 20 years. You don't have to do anything to earn appreciation, which is where the big dollars come from. In other words, if I make $500 cash flow a month on a property, that's $6,000 a year—but if your property worth $200,000 appreciates 5% in one year, that's $10,000! You don't have to do anything to earn appreciation, which is where the big dollars come from.

Let's say you want to earn $10,000 per month. Each unit or home will have cash flows of $100-$500. You don't want to count on the property appreciating, but you do want to count on your investments being positive at the end of each month. Take your goal of $10,000 and divide it by $300 to get approximately 33. This number means you would need 33 units to reach your goal of having $10,000 a month in cash flow. This may seem like a lot at first, but if you make this a three-to-five-year goal and start buying multiple units, you'll get there before you know it!

Always remember the old saying that we overestimate what can get done in one year and underestimate what can get done in three years. If you buy three units a year, you'll have 33 within 10 years—and it will likely be even sooner as you take advantage of taxes and appreciation. Also, making $300 per unit is a conservative goal. I generally make at least $700 per unit, which means to hit the goal of a $10,000 monthly cash flow, I would only need 17 units. On my short-term rentals, I make a minimum of $1,500 per unit. With only seven properties at that return, I earn $10,500 per month.

Before investing, you always have to research the neighborhood, city, state laws and numbers. You could, for example, purchase in a state with high property taxes (like Texas) or a state with low property taxes (like Wyoming), and the numbers will be dramatically different in either scenario. If you live in an area with hurricanes, the cost of insurance coverage may increase—

the same is true if you purchase near a body of water or flood zone. Another variable to consider is the age of the property. If you buy brand-new construction, you're not going to have a lot of deferred maintenance while a building from 1900 will have a lot of charm...and expenses.

Not All Debt is Bad (A Secret of the Rich)

You were likely taught that all debt is bad, but you weren't told that there are various types of debt, especially in real estate, that actually grow your assets. As long as you aren't over-leveraged (meaning the loans you take out are so big that you can't pay them off), you can use loans to make more money on your own funds as well as the bank's money. Pretty cool, right? The most successful real estate investors take out big loans, so they are highly leveraged. That's good debt! (Note: this is a theme I am repeating from a previous chapter because it is so important!)

An example of bad debt is spending excessively on credit cards. If you eat out every meal, buy expensive clothes, drive a new luxury car with a high monthly payment or rent a house of equal to more than half of your income, you're likely going to incur a lot of bad debt.

With good debt, of course, you must understand how to mitigate risk and borrow according to your comfort level. If your comfort level is holding you back from expanding, however, you'll want to find a happy medium to stretch yourself a bit toward growth without being completely stressed out.

What about student loan debt? I don't recommend that you pay it all off right away. I knew an attorney who ended up paying off all her student loans after making a few great real estate deals. She didn't have the debt hanging over her, but she also had no way to grow her income. If your loan is 4% and you can make 15% on your real estate investment, there might be a good argument for making the minimum payments on your student loans while leveraging what you make from your investment. Simply put, *utilizing* debt is one of the key ways people get rich.

Let's take a look at the power of leveraging. For example, on a $200,000 property, you only put $40,000 down (or 20%) and you're making money on the entire loan—which you borrowed for less than 5% interest. If you're earning 10% a year and borrowing at 5%, you're making a hefty profit! I always recommend leveraging as long as you're using after-tax dollars.

There's a way to get a loan inside your 401(k), but the interest rates are high. One company to look into on this topic is www.nasb.com. As you continue to follow your opportunities for growth, you should entertain every option.

Your properties gain equity as you pay down your monthly loans. Then, as properties go up in value with appreciation, you will want to use some of that money to purchase another property. Remember that when you take the equity out of a property, it's called a cash out refinance. You refinance your mortgage for a new one with a larger amount so that you can use your mortgage to obtain cash.

For example, if you own a home worth $500,000 that is paid in full, you can get $400,000 in cash out, or 75% of the property's value, as long as you qualify. A refinance is brilliant in that way, because it's tax-deferred income that you only owe taxes on once you sell the property. Now, you have that money to go buy additional properties! Real estate offers many tax incentives, and working with a great CPA or exploring other options in this book will help you offset your income and avoid taxes.

You have four ways to multiply your profits in addition to cash flow:

1. Paying down the loan and gaining equity.
2. Gaining through appreciation.
3. Doing a cash out refinance.
4. Saving money through tax advantages.

When these four strategies work together, you are maximizing your ability to make your dollars grow.

You will make the most money in real estate by using leveraged strategies like these. I want to drive this point home, so here is another example: if you only have $100,000 to invest, you can borrow $400,000 and put 25% down on a property valued at $500,000. The loan enables you to make money not only on your own, but on what you borrow!

This is the basic strategy of the top 1% of wealth-makers. Most people are afraid to use this method because they've been taught that all debt is bad. They believe that they might end up losing all of their money—but now that you're reading this book, you know better.

Differences in Loan Terms

For one-to-four-unit properties, your loan amount is typically based on how much income you'll make from renting the property. The lender generally looks at your W-2 and your last two income tax returns, and there's a debt-to-income ratio that you must meet in order to qualify for the loan. For one-to-four-units, you'll apply for a conventional loan. For this, the lender will look at comparable properties in the area to estimate the value of the property you want to buy. So, if houses are all selling for $100,000, they're going to loan you a certain amount up to that value—usually 75-80%.

To assess what that value is, professional appraisers come in and evaluate the square footage of the property, comparing it to what other similar properties in the area have sold for. If the property is decorated and rehabbed beautifully, that can affect your resale price, but it will not matter for the appraisal. If the property you're buying is in unlivable condition and can't be rented out in its current state, you won't be able to get a traditional loan.

Traditional banks won't lend you money on a property where they aren't convinced you can rent and cover your mortgage. Not to worry! You can borrow money outside of a bank for a property in any condition—you can even borrow money for raw land! The loan interest will be higher, but it may be worth the investment in the long run. Whenever you buy a property, the lender always has the note on the property until the loan is fully repaid, while you carry the grant deed (which gives you the right of ownership).

Different Types of Loans

Unless you're using a commercial loan (for more than five units) or plan to sell the property in a few years, don't use a variable loan, which has a fluctuating interest rate over time. You will want to know what the bank expects you to pay in total and per month.

Loans must go through underwriting and aren't confirmed until the lender's final approval. Even after you give all of your paperwork to the lender, the person administering the loan is going to collect all of your paperwork and submit it for official approval. The underwriters will crunch the numbers and inevitably ask for a lot of additional verification on the details.

Recourse Versus Non-Recourse Loans

Depending on whether the lender is an independent broker and owner of the company or works for a large firm, they may have flexibility on interest rates. By shopping around, I have saved up to $24,000 on loans up front. It takes a bit of extra effort, but it's worth it.

These days, you can use a Google calculator to figure out your mortgage rate average. The key word here, however, is "average." There are a lot of variables that go into the rate of a loan, and not all lenders will require the same information or charge the same rate.

There are all sorts of lenders and types of loans that we've discussed previously. Additionally, you may qualify for a veteran loan or an FHA loan for little to no money down. One of the most common is a government agency loan through Fannie Mae or Freddie Mac, which are government-backed agencies that allow you to obtain non-recourse loans. If you end up defaulting on a non-recourse loan, you can walk away from the house without owing the balance of the loan. The same isn't true of a recourse loan, however.

Thirty-Year Fixed Loans

I mentioned this type of loan earlier in the book. This is the best loan ever, and the United States is the only place in the world that offers a loan for 30 years that never adjusts with inflation. It's an amazing way to make your money work for you, but it only works for properties with one to four units. Let's say you borrow $80,000 today on a property. During that 30 years, your property will appreciate, but your loan won't increase. These loans are generally offered by Fannie Mae and Freddie Mac and are backed by the government. However, these agency lenders have created the restriction that only 10 of these loans are allowed per person, to prevent investors from taking advantage by buying up every property and locking in the lowest available rate for 30 years.

Fifteen-Year Loan

Due to the shorter duration, your interest rate for a 15-year loan will be higher. The advantage is that the property is paid off in 15 years instead of 30. Some investors prefer this loan because once it's paid off, all of the money they were using to pay the loan becomes cash flow. At a certain point, some investors no longer want debt.

Remember, however, that while you're cutting 15 years off the life of your loan, you're going to have to pay more each month. You'll also lose that additional 15 years of inflation that you would save on a 30-year loan. So it's something to consider if you're working on growing wealth. You want the loan to last as long as possible to meet that objective.

This concept can be hard to understand. With real estate, you need to learn how to adjust your mind to project returns and true costs in the future. If you pay off your property in 15 years, you will have no more payments, which is great—but if you keep the loan over time, you'll actually save more money. I always like to remind myself of the avocado that costs more today than it did 30 years ago!

Interest-Only, 5-7-10-Year Balloon Loans, Adjustable-Rate Mortgages and Commercial Loans

These loans offer fixed rates for a certain number of years with prepayment penalties or variable rates for a set period depending on the market and the terms of the loan. Commercial loans are given this way; you likely won't get a 30-year fixed and have many loan options. The best one will depend on your strategy for the acquisition. You can often get the most favorable rates by working with local banks.

Always shop around for interest rates and calculate where you project the rates may move in the future. Remember, the interest rate can fluctuate, and before the term expires, the loan needs to be renegotiated, paid in full or the property needs to be sold.

Amortization is the process of spreading a loan into payments that consist of both principal and interest over a set period of time. It allows you to gradually write off the initial cost of an asset over a period of time.

You will get various options with commercial loans on five units or more in a property. You can even pay interest-only, which means no principal, which is very common if you're doing renovations. This enables you to keep your payments low when your expenses are high. You can also get loans locked at certain rates with extension options and varying amortization tables (which lay out how much money needs to be paid over a given period of time).

Commercial loans are used for mobile home parks, storage units, apartments and retail properties. These investments are calculated on a cap rate, which is the amount of income the units generate from the rent minus the expenses. Because there are many units and larger numbers involved, the calculations can be very complex. The loan is awarded and calculated by your ability to make the payments, based on your investment.

In this case, the income you generate from a W-2 or tax return isn't part of the equation. With these loans, the lender also doesn't look at comparable properties. The only factor is what they believe the property income will generate and your ability to pay back the loan.

If you want to jump into buying large buildings, you may need to take on a principal partner. This person gets a piece of the deal in exchange for co-signing the documents and backing the deal. They generally have a lot of money, experience in working with the asset class and a relation-ship with a bank offering the loan.

Private and Hard Money Loans

If you're doing a flip and need money for a home that's in bad shape, you'll need to use hard money from a private lender. As I've mentioned, these are non-bank lenders who can create any guidelines they want. Properties that are in bad shape are considered a higher risk. The lender is able to make terms that reflect that risk by asking for more money for the deal. Also, if it's your first or second deal, the lender may charge more based on your inexperience. After a few deals, you can negotiate more favorable terms.

I've told you about getting large sums of money quickly for a higher interest rate. A hard money lender can charge anywhere from 8-12% annualized plus several points, which are charged on the purchase price of the property. Two points on a $100,000 purchase would be 2%, or $2,000 of additional money.

Most lenders don't want to provide a loan for a small return such as $2,000 if you hold the loan for only a month. So, to ensure they make some decent money, they will charge up to four points up front or create a minimum hold time guarantee. On the $200,000 loan held for a month, they would then make $8,000, which is four points or 4%. The terms make a huge difference. Losing $8,000 on the deal may sound like a lot of money, but if you stand to make $30,000 from your investment, it's worth it. You have to crunch the numbers to determine if your returns will be worth the hefty cost of the loan.

When you first enter the real estate investing world, you may wonder where to find these lenders. The truth is that once you start attending local meetups and talking to other investors on networking websites, you'll meet many people who do this sort of lending. The reason they're willing to take the risk on these rehab deals is that they frequently require you to pay the points up front. That way, they're getting a chunk of money right away while also obtaining the note for the property, and they receive your property as collateral.

Seller Finance

When the owner decides to loan you the money to buy the property and requests a certain amount in a lump sum up front, it's called seller finance. I often get the question, "Why would a seller agree to loan you the money on a sale of their own property?" The answer is that in some cases, the seller can negotiate a higher sales price and save big on sales taxes by doing so.

Let's say the seller purchased a rental property for $100,000 and it was used as an investment. With a current value of $300,000, and considering that it was used as an investment property, that $200,000 profit would be taxed at close to 40%! If the seller takes their profit over time, they can dramatically lower their tax burden.

In other words, if the owner just sold their property,

they would have to pay tax on $200,000 that same year. If they did a seller finance deal, the buyer would pay the seller slowly every month over a duration of time. That way, the seller would get a steady income stream on a monthly basis, and if the buyer ended up defaulting on the loan, the seller could take the property back (because they would still have the property note as collateral). Because the terms are so favorable for the buyer, they are sometimes willing to pay a bit more for the investment.

For a more detailed study of this idea, read *The Book on Investing in Real Estate with No (and Low) Money Down* by Brandon Turner of *Bigger Pockets*. Most of the deals I'm talking about in this book for beginning investors will be done more conventionally, but I certainly want you to at least know the basics of these different options. When you don't have any money, investing can require more legwork—but more advantageous situations like this one are most definitely possible.

Is It a Good Deal?

Estimating the variables you can't control will always guide your final decision on an investment. For example, if a house gives you an approximate 10% profit annually and the mitigated risks are low, then it is a great deal. If the profit is estimated at 20% annually but the risk for issues is high, you might want to take a pass.

The risks vary depending on many factors, including

the location, price of purchase, cost of repairs and how much you can get for rent. With all these variables in mind, you can't entirely predict every factor. You may not know that the HVAC unit will break, for example, but if it's more than 15 years old, that's certainly a likely possibility. You could also rent to a tenant who ends up not paying the rent because they lost their job. The list can go on and on. If you calculate the cost of those items, you can anticipate them and leave some extra room in your budget. That way, when something happens that you truly *can't* anticipate, you'll usually still come out ahead.

Always factor in property taxes, utilities and Homeowners Association (HOA) fees when applicable. These can all make a huge difference in your profit. In most states, property taxes are reassessed when you buy, and there are different advantages to navigating each guideline.

In California, there's Proposition 13, which locks in property taxes at the time of purchase. As a result, my mother still pays $700 in tax per year for the property she bought 45 years ago for $65,000. When she sells the property, the new owner will pay closer to $7,000 annually based on its property value today. Additionally, if my mom transferred the property to my name or decided to sell the property, she would owe taxes on $500,000 (Note: the capital gains exemption could've been an option if she had lived in the property for two of the last five years—that exemption is worth $250,000 for a single person or $500,000 for a married couple). At this point, my mother's biggest tax advantage is not to sell the property and to leave it in a living trust to her children or grandchildren, who will then take advantage of a step up in cost basis.

A new cost basis is established based on the value of the property when it gets transferred upon death. So, if my mom bought the property for $65,000 and decides to leave it to my kids, they will only pay tax on the difference between the $650,000 value and the current sale price, *not* on her $65,000 original purchase price.

Don't ever try and convince yourself that a deal is good if the numbers say it isn't. Even if there's potential for high returns, don't take the deal if the risk is too great. It's better to pass on a property if the numbers don't show you that you can make it work in your favor.

It's a good idea to ask an expert for support to make sure you're on the right track, go over the numbers with someone you trust or hire a mentor. Of course, always remember that there are variables you can't control, so sometimes your numbers may still not add up the way you anticipated. Most great real estate investors have had this experience, so don't beat yourself up over it. You can still potentially make a killing on the next deal, so just keep adding up your numbers and forge ahead.

Real estate investing is a matter of taking action steps while obtaining knowledge and strategy with the numbers. If you want to grow wealth, you have to get comfortable with the unknown variables and be willing to take calculated risks.

The 70% Rule

The 70% rule states that an investor should pay no more than 70% of the After-Repair Value (ARV) of a property minus the repairs needed. The ARV is an estimate of what a home is worth after it's fully repaired, and it's the calculation that's generally used with rehabilitated properties.

Let's break it down: if you estimate that a property's ARV will be $150,000, this means that you should spend no more than $105,000 on the property—70% of $150,000 is $105,000. This is a great way to get a ballpark figure. If I pay $105,000 for a property and spend $80,000 on repairs, it isn't a profitable deal.

At 70%, your strike price is 0.7 times the after-repair value minus the rehabilitation cost. So, let's look at an example of that another way. If your ARV (After Repair Value) is $150,000 and the rehab cost is $25,000, you would calculate your 70% as 0.7 times the purchase price minus $25,000. The sum of that is $80,000, which would be the purchase amount you would offer for the property. If you wanted to give yourself more padding to make sure you could pay for the rehab and make a profit, you would offer a bit less.

You will analyze a lot of deals, and most of them won't

work. That's fine; just pass on those until you find one that will. It's all part of the process.

Calculating Cap Rates

Capitalization rates (or cap rates) are how you determine the value and potential return on an investment. These rates are usually used to analyze income-producing properties of more than four units, multi-family properties and commercial loans. One-to-four units are based on appraisals and comparable recent sales in the neighborhood in terms of size and square footage.

Calculating Cap Rates

Let's say you're looking at a 10-unit property for a million dollars, and the cap rate is 6%. That 6% cap rate is calculated by dividing the property's Net Operating Income (NOI) by the current market value. Note that the cap rate doesn't include the mortgage in the calculation because loan rates fluctuate, and the buyer doesn't know what kind of rate and terms they're going to get. The 6% can be deceiving because you might think it's 6% *all in*, but it isn't. To know your true operating expenses, you have to adjust the calculation to include the loan.

What is a Good Rate of Return on a Property?

As I've said, I like to get a 10-12% cash-on-cash return for an investment. It's very good and very ambitious. I don't always reach that number, but often, I do even better. In a market where the properties are appreciating, the annual rate of return for cash flow is generally lower. It could be as low as 3-5%. For example, in Austin, Texas where I live, prices are high and rents can't keep up with those prices. After all expenses are paid on a property, there isn't much left for cash flow unless you use the furnished rental model like Airbnb. (As previously mentioned, some counties have rules that restrict short-term rental properties, so be sure to check!)

Syndication deals usually pay a 7-9% preferred return and 17-20% annualized. Remember that with these deals, you're a passive investor, meaning you do no work. Passive investing is popular because an investor can make almost the same money for no work as they would managing an investment. Since I said I was happy with 12%, passive investing works well for me. If you don't have as much capital to invest, however, you may need to do a bit more of the work yourself.

Part of what makes a syndication work is investing at least $25,000 into a deal. Depending on how it's set up, you may need to show that you're an accredited investor. This means you must have a net worth of one million dollars or earn $200,000 as a single person (or $300,000 as a married couple) annually.

If you are ready to invest in a syndication and don't know where to start, visit my website at:

www.wealthbuildingconcierge.com

Using the 1% Rule

The 1% rule can be used as a rough guideline to determine if your property will be profitable. The calculation is simple: 1% of a $100,000 purchase is $1,000 a month. This number will almost guarantee a cash flow of $100-$300 or more per month. However, that amount of cash flow isn't enough to move the needle on your financial freedom number. As I mentioned in the last chapter, you'll either need to purchase a few hundred units or come up with a strategy that will get your cash flowing sooner. If you buy properties under value that are distressed (or if you can rent them furnished for a premium), you can make more money per unit on each property.

The 1% rule is monthly rental income equal to at least 1% of the purchase price.

You can also work to get deals at a discount to increase

your profit margin. To get a better purchase price or cap rate on a property, investors often reach out to small business owners (often referred to as "mom and pop" owners). It's possible to negotiate directly with them. You can also send out mailers or run ads to find distressed sellers—these are usually people who recently lost a job, are getting divorced, have had a death in the family or simply ran out of money.

An area with more cash flow will generally be in a less expensive neighborhood, while you'll see more appreciation in popular areas or neighborhoods that are building up. For example, in Los Angeles or Austin, the cap rate will be lower, at about 3-5%. In cash flowing areas, it could be more like 7-10%.

You always want to find a way to maximize your profits. With each investment, you will get better at figuring out ways to make more money the next time around, all while growing your portfolio. Look at every variable you can think of before making an offer on a property or partnering in someone else's deal. The numbers will always be a key indicator in determining whether or not a deal will work for you. Other ways to improve the numbers include adding value to increase rents or negotiating a better rate on your loan. It's a creative process that is ever-evolving.

Bear in mind that you will make mistakes from time to time, especially when you're starting out. As you do more deals, your bag of real estate investing tricks will grow. Remember that you can even do deals without using any of your own money. When you do invest your own dollars, start challenging yourself to see how quickly you can get the invested funds returned. The ability to reinvest your money can make a difference in your bottom-line returns.

How Fast Do You Get Your Initial Investment Returned?

Your initial investment is called your principal. If I use $100,000 to buy a property, I need to calculate my return with the expectation of getting that money back as soon as possible. The longer it takes to get back your principal affects your opportunity cost, because you won't have those funds to reinvest. The opportunity cost takes into account the amount of time your money is invested, and you can't use it for any other deal.

For instance, if I loan you $5,000 and you pay me back in three years, it will be a better return for me than if you pay me back in 10 years. You will become more aware of this number if you decide to invest in syndication deals.

Some opportunities in syndication deals provide longer hold times than others. You will often see a range in the projected hold period, such as five to seven years or seven to 10 years. Sometimes, there are refinances after two years, which will get you back around 65% of your principal. The refinance enables the sponsor to take money out of the deal based on the increase in value after the improvements have been made to the property. It's the same idea as the BRRR strategy, but on a larger scale.

As soon as you get your initial investment returned, you can take the money and put it into other deals to multiply your profits. You don't have to pay taxes on the money until the sale of a property, so a refinance also gives you more time to make money. Unless you plan a tax advantage strategy, the taxes will all be due at the time of sale. One way people avoid paying fees is by deferring them through a 1031 exchange (more on that shortly).

How Do You Calculate the Profit on a Property?

There are four areas to review to understand the basic calculations. Take a sheet of paper and divide it into four columns. The first column is your income. This includes rents, laundry, storage facility and parking garage. The second column is all of your expenses. The third column is your cash flow, which is your income minus your expenses. The fourth column is the cash-on-cash return on your investment. You have to add your down payment, closing costs and the rehab budget to the purchase price. It's the total amount of money you put in the deal, divided by the annual cash flow. That will be your cash-on-cash return.

Let's say you bought a property for $100,000, and you're earning $1,000 a month in income. Make that column one. In the second column place mortgage, utilities, repairs and the gardener, which amounts to $600 each month. When you subtract $600 (expenses) from $1,000 (income) you have $400 in column three, which is your cash flow. Your last column shows you the profitability of your property based on your initial investment (this is cash-on-cash return). You put down 20% of $100,000 ($20,000) plus $6,000 for closing and $8,500 for rehab. Your total investment is $34,500. Take your annualized income of $4,800 ($400 a month cash flow times 12) and divide by $34,500 to get .139 or a little less than 14%. (I didn't subtract any money for repairs or vacancies, but $1,000 could have been deducted from the cash flow.)

Income	Expenses	Cash Flow	$\dfrac{4,800}{34,500} =$	cash-on-cash return -139 or 13%
$1,000	$600	$400.00		

Wherever you look for a property, you still need to check the same variables. First, review the asking price and what you think the property is worth. Determine if it's in an area that's appreciating, there are forced appreciation opportunities or you can get cash flow (if that's your goal).

Remember that forced appreciation is when you buy a property at a discount so that you'll have equity or profit in it out of the gate, or when you make improvements that raise its value. In other words, if I find a property that I think is worth $100,000 but I buy it for $70,000, I'll be receiving $30,000 of forced appreciation. If I can fix up the place with paint for $5,000, I will still have $25,000 more value than what I paid for it, making it a total of $25,000 forced appreciation after expenses.

Value additions to a property are a huge way to create profit. These include adding a bedroom, converting a garage, remodeling kitchens or bathrooms, changing floors, painting and landscaping. Overall, statistics show that the master bedroom, landscaping and kitchens tend to give you the most profit back for your money. You don't want to redo a kitchen for $30,000, however, if you can't sell the property for at least $35,000 more than your investment as a result of the improvement. All of the rehab costs and calculations must be figured into your final offer and proposal to the seller.

The likelihood of losing your money, especially if you're able to hold onto the investment for any length of time, is almost zero. This doesn't mean that you will have access to the funds during that period or that you won't go negative at some point. The investment has a projection of time to make a certain amount, but once again, you need to plan reserves in the event that the market shifts. Even if the market does shift, however, it will inevitably rebound and come back stronger than the decline. Nevertheless, that can take some time.

Deferred Maintenance

The year a property was built can make a huge difference in how much maintenance and repairs will cost. In general, an older building will need more repairs with greater frequency. Deferred maintenance is a term used for neglected or older buildings where the owners may have never changed any plumbing, or that may have a 20-year-old roof. While gutters only need to be cleaned maybe once a year, if you have a property with lots of trees and gutters that have never been cleaned, it could cost a lot to clean them.

That said, old buildings have a lot of charm, so people love to rent them. Most people anticipate the maintenance but are willing to pay the cost for the charm factor. If you want to buy such a property, you just need a substantial cushion for unforeseen repairs.

Keep Thinking Long Term

My first property is now worth $1.4 million. I recently took money out of it for a second time to buy another property in a cash-out refinance. My rents are still paid by my tenants, and the value continues to grow. This allows me to repeat the process with more properties.

Think for just a moment of the alternative. Had I not purchased that property, the $40,000 I saved could have been used for a first-class ticket to Europe and a few Gucci bags. I could have also kept it in a savings account while I continued to pay monthly rent. How much would that money be worth today if I had made those choices? Certainly not as much as my property has afforded me! So always, always think long term!

Chapter 6 Actions

1. Run the numbers on three properties, including income (rental income, laundry, storage and miscellaneous), cash flow (income - expenses = cash flow) and expenses (taxes and utilities including water, electric, garbage and sewer; HOA; gardening or snow removal; possible vacancy; repairs; appliance replacements; property manager and mortgage).

2. What are the risks with each purchase? What is the cash flow on each property analyzed?

3. Look at your numbers, math and money fears. On a scale of one to 10, where do you place yourself? How can you tweak your thinking to bypass your emotional or mental obstacles and move towards your goals?

SEVEN
MAKE OFFERS, BUY AND CLOSE

> *Strong women don't play victim, don't make themselves look pitiful and don't point the finger. They stand and they deal.*
> —Mandy Hale

You are getting closer to getting the deal. The contract is almost in your hot little hands, and growing your wealth is imminent. Now, it's time to acquire a property.

If you're looking for properties to purchase now, you're on the right track. Email me at hello@wealthbuildingconcierge.com to let me know you're looking or tag me @wealthbuildingconcierge on Instagram. If you're in a place where you want more support, visit my website at:

www.weathbuildingconcierge.com

Once you're there, you can fill out an application to work with me. Remember, it doesn't matter where you are in the process. What matters is that you ask how and move forward!

Are You Ready to Buy?

Heck, yes. Finding a property is work, but it gets easier as you gain experience. Once you find a location you think is promising, visit the destination or area and find a realtor. Next, look for a team to do repairs. Look for property managers, contact the owners and connect with a network in the area.

If you're working with a realtor, they will walk you through the buying and closing process, but I can't tell you how empowering it is to understand the process on your own. That way, if something comes up that doesn't feel or look right to you, you'll have the knowledge to question it and walk through the transaction more cautiously. When you're signing documents, make sure you understand all of the details. If you don't, this is where your team can come in.

All offers need to be presented to the seller. Generally, the seller has three days to accept or counter your offer, and you can make more than one offer to a seller. With a seller finance deal, you can offer more money and different terms than your first offer. After your offer is accepted, you will still have three days to cancel, but if you're speaking directly with the seller, you can set the duration and terms.

When negotiating directly with a seller, it's common to make them more than one offer because you're trying to accommodate both their needs and yours. To do so, try to find out what's important to the seller. If you're buying a home for yourself and your family, for example, write a letter with your offer to share why the house is perfect for you. Personalizing your offer can really give you some leverage, especially in cases where a family is moving out and they like the idea of a new family moving in and making memories. These sales are personal, so get the kids and the dog!

How Do You Find Sellers?

You can go the traditional route and get a realtor to use the MLS (Multiple Listing Service, a site that lists properties being sold by realtors). Sometimes, sellers want to sell the property themselves, which is called "for sale by owner." As I've said, to get off-market deals, you often need to find distressed sellers who eagerly need or want to sell their property. Sometimes, that can be as simple as older people who are ready to retire.

They often don't have mortgages, so they can sell the property at a discount and still make a sizable profit. For example, if a couple bought their home for $300,000 and now owe nothing on it, every dollar they get minus taxes will go into their pocket. It makes getting $250,000 still feel like a large amount of money.

At first, it may feel daunting to contact distressed sellers, but they're usually quite grateful, because they're looking for help to get out of their situation. Public records with the city or websites that collect data on these types of sellers are great places to start. That way, you can see if they haven't paid their property taxes or if they only owe a a little bit more on their mortgage. You can also get this information from a company like Property Radar or Prop Stream.

To get the phone numbers of the owners, you can use what's called "skip tracing"—try Clear Skip or Call Porter for this, and then call, send letters or text. You can even knock on their door! It sounds strange, but this can be an effective way to find an off-market opportunity. Pursuing the off-market route can take time and effort, but if you're set on getting a discounted price, it is a good avenue to pursue.

You can also scream from the mountaintop, "I want to buy real estate!" In other words, tell everyone you know the kind of property you're looking for, your budget and how they can support you.

Be strategic. If you want to buy a property with a realtor but you know other people are making high offers, try to come up with more desirable terms in order to get the deal.

How Much Should You Offer?

This question comes up a lot, and there are many variables that determine what makes a good offer. Again, look at comparable properties when you're buying one-to-four units. Comprehensive data means that you compare square footage, amenities and what has sold in the area recently. In other words, no one will buy a home for $200,000 more than what three similar homes sold for up the street. Once you're dealing with multi-family properties, you'll be looking more at cap rates and the net income the property produces and is projected to produce.

Answer these questions:

- Are you planning to buy and hold the property or sell it right away?
- How much profit is in the deal?
- At what point would the property no longer be a good deal for you?
- How much time do you need to put in to make the investment profitable?
- Will the investment meet your objectives?

You may decide that you won't pay a dollar over a certain amount. If you think the property is $75,000 under value and the seller is asking for $200,000, would you pay $215,000? Remember that it's worth $275,000.

You need to ask yourself if it makes sense to pay an extra $15,000 to get the deal. Think about it: we can get stubborn about the price if we feel like we're overpaying, but there are times when paying a bit more makes sense.

Another factor you need to consider is how much demand there is for the property. If it's a good deal, unless you're the first one there and no competition is present, you're competing with lots of offers. Demand will drive up the purchase price.

Avoiding the crowds of people going for the same property is the reason why lots of people work to get in direct contact with sellers to make a deal. Once a property is listed on the MLS, it isn't as likely you'll be able to negotiate a deal directly with the seller, so it's best to reach them before they list their property.

If you can find the sellers who are willing to make deals with you without a lot of other people around, you can offer less than market value. Sometimes, you may want to offer more in a competitive market if you feel the opportunity is a great deal. If you're willing to do what others won't to find a deal, you'll be able to find more of them.

In the long run, it's best when both the buyer and the seller are happy. A few thousand dollars won't make a significant difference in the grand scheme of things. There are even times when you'll pay substantially more than the asking price, and it still may be worth it.

You don't want to chase a deal once it goes from great

to *way* overpriced, however. At the point that you no longer feel confident about the price, wait for the next opportunity. It will inevitably come—especially when you're looking. Again, before you make an offer, always do your due diligence with an inspection, and check the property to make sure there are no expenses that haven't been accounted for.

Making an offer can feel intimidating, but it isn't that complicated. You're looking to get two parties to agree to terms that work for each of them. As I've said, if you're making a deal for a private home or you have a connection to the property, I always recommend writing a personal letter about what the property means to you or would mean to you. This may be the only chance you get to meet the owners. My husband and I bought our house with eight other offers on the table, and ours won because the owner liked our letter!

I even have quite a few friends who have been able to purchase large portfolios at a deep discount because they found a mom and pop who wanted to sell to someone they liked more than they wanted to get every dollar out of the deal.

Make Several Offers

You may not often see advice that tells you to bid on multiple properties at the same time, especially since most people only want to buy one property—but you're an investor! If you get more than one property, you can see if someone else wants to buy it from you in a wholesaling deal, or you can just decline the deal. The likelihood that you'll find multiple properties at the same time and have them all accepted is very low. It would actually be a great problem to have! And if you want to buy more than one, you can always find partners. If it's truly a great deal, I would look for opportunities to find the money, and I would try to buy low and sell high whenever possible. The bottom line is that sometimes you need to make a lot of offers before getting a deal at a price you want.

Organization and Paperwork

I will be the first to admit that organizing is boring and cumbersome. I have scoured my computer and desk for papers many times over the years. It still happens today at times, although less frequently.

Nevertheless, it's important for bigger issues like audits and taxes to organize all of your documents, and it's frustrating to waste valuable time searching for papers because you haven't created a good filing system.

Once you start to build a portfolio of several properties, organization becomes even more important. So, make your life easier, and hire help if you need it. You'll save yourself a big headache in the long run. Also, automate everything you can to save time and for efficiency.

Lease Options

A lease option is another type of offer you can make. This agreement gives the renter a choice to purchase the rented property at the beginning, during or at the end of the rental period. It also precludes the owner from offering the property for sale to anyone else. When the term expires, the renter must either exercise the option or forfeit the deposit. The lease option generally requires the potential buyer to pay for all of the repairs and may also ask them for a fee for the option to buy the home.

If you're living in a house for a while and the owner decides to sell it, they may want to sell it to you because they know and like you. If you're living in a rental home, you can always ask the owner if they want to sell the property to you before they've even thought about selling it!

Liens

When the seller has not paid certain bills, the person who is owed money puts a lien on the property to make sure they get paid in full when the property is sold.

If the property is sold through foreclosure or wholesalers, the wholesaler or bank will often check for liens prior to selling it. If those liens are missed and you buy the property, you'll have to pay off the liens yourself! You can often obtain information about liens in public records, so just make sure you don't end up surprised.

A clean title means there are no liens. If there are some, you can request they be paid by the seller prior to your taking over the property, or you can agree to pay the liens if the deal still makes sense. For example, if I'm buying a house worth $400,000 for $200,000 and it has $50,000 in liens, the numbers still work!

Rents

How much a property will rent for is one of the key factors to calculate when making an offer. Positive attributes that add value to a property include a great location, good schools nearby and how nice the place looks. You can start by looking at Craigslist or Zillow to see what rents go for in the area, or you can talk to a property manager or realtor.

I like a website called Rentometer, which gives you the 25th percentile, median price and 75th percentile for rents in a given area. If you're going to be in the higher bracket, it likely means you will have to remodel the property to ensure it has a nice kitchen and a good layout. If you furnish it, I recommend doubling the listed long-term rental rate to see if it's a property worth purchasing. If it's in a high demand area, you can drive those prices up even more.

Inspections

I've mentioned inspections a few times, but what else do you need to know about this important part of the process? Make sure the professional inspector checks pools, septic tanks, foundations and possible termite infestation. Those features are sometimes not included in a standard inspection.

For best results, come along for the inspection or call the inspector afterwards to talk about the property. If you still like the property after the inspector says there are issues, you can go back to the seller and request credits, but understand that they don't have to agree with your request. Still, you can ask and negotiate. These are repair credits, which are often given to offset the costs you'll incur while fixing things after you buy the property.

Sometimes, your lender will want some repairs to be done before you close on the property, particularly if it's termite work. This helps them to safeguard their loan to you. If there are a lot of backup offers from other buyers, however, avoid being overly demanding of credits because the seller can decide to move on to the next offer.

The inspection period is also a great time to drive by the building at night and make sure it feels safe. This step is very important, as I have abandoned several deals after finding issues with them after inspection.

A Note About "As-Is"

When a seller writes "as is" about a property in an ad, don't assume you have no negotiating power. This is an indication that the seller wants to do business with someone who will take the property without any questions. But once you're under contract together and negotiating, you can always dance and potentially get a further discount or some repair credits.

Saving Money on the Offer

Remember that the seller always pays for the buyer's real estate agent as well as the seller's agent (unless they list for sale without a realtor). You can obtain your own real estate license, however, and represent yourself, which means you can keep the realtor fee for buying or selling.

You can also hire an attorney to go over the paperwork for you. If you're selling a property as "for sale by owner," you can pay a realtor a flat fee to post your property in the MLS. The MLS will give you the most visibility, but you can only access that list with a real estate license.

How and When to Make an Offer

After you crunch your numbers, choose your strategy and find a deal, it's time to make an offer to acquire the property. I know this can feel a bit scary. You're taking a leap to put money down and make an investment, and you're opening yourself up to a world of variables that can transpire with property ownership. You could lose money! But remember: you could also *make* money!

There are several ways offers can be made. If you're working with a realtor, they will make the offer on your behalf, but you don't have to work with a realtor or have a real estate license to purchase real estate. You can also make an offer as an individual. If you go this route, I recommend that you have an escrow company or attorney to act as a middle person for the exchange of funds and documents between you and the seller. This will protect your money and your interests.

When you write an offer on your own for a seller without a realtor, it doesn't need to be in accordance with the rules of the real estate board. It's up to the two of you to make the deal work. All agreements must be in writing and signed by both parties. Often, there's a minimal earnest money deposit exchanged to make the contract binding as well.

Keep in mind that whenever you purchase a property, the seller has a goal in mind. They're selling because they're moving somewhere else, can no longer afford the home, recently had someone pass away or are investing like you. Write your offer accommodating whatever that seller's need is. In many cases, you can simply ask the seller what their desired outcome is from the sale, whether it's to sell by a certain date or to get a certain amount of money. If you can accommodate them, you have a much better chance of closing the deal.

An Offer is Just an Offer

The other day, a friend of mine told me she was working on a flip and an older gentleman was at his home next door, mowing the lawn. She looked at his house, envisioning what it would look like with the porch redone and a fresh coat of paint. The old man looked at my friend and asked, "Do you like my house?" She said that she did. "Do you want to buy it?"

Right there, they made a deal that she would take over the bank payments and pay him 6% interest on the loan. He was renting the place for $500 when the market rate was $1,000. Not only did my friend make instant cash flow, but she got herself a property. Situations like this don't always happen often, but they do happen!

The bottom line is: don't be afraid to make offers. People can ignore you or say no, but every offer brings you closer to a yes! As with any negotiation, however, you're looking to make the best deal for both parties. Just don't get so invested in how much you want the property that you taint your ability to be objective and stick to the numbers. If you pay too much, you won't achieve your goal of making money.

Be First in Line and Ready to Do Business

In a competitive market, coming in with cash to make an offer and close quickly is another way to beat out the competition. (Once a seller accepts your offer, they can take backup offers in the event you cancel the contract.)

Sellers want to do business with someone they think will close. Regardless of what the terms are, everybody wants to do business with someone they know is serious and can actually execute the deal, so be very clear about your terms. Present a strong, solid offer and be on top of everything so the seller feels confident about you. Pay attention to deadlines and details throughout the process so you don't miss anything.

Bear in mind that there are certain times when you can't get your down payment refunded, causing you to lose money if you suddenly want out of a deal. So check on these timelines carefully!

Earnest Money Versus Option Money

When you make an offer on a property, there are earnest money and option money fees that you must pay within three days of your offer's acceptance. Option fees are paid directly to the seller and are only refundable at closing; in other words, if you don't close on the property, they're non-refundable. You can give as low as $5 for option fees, but if you're willing to give $500+, it's a way of showing the seller you really want the property and aren't planning on backing out of the deal.

Earnest money is typically paid to the title insurance company for the seller and held in escrow. These are good faith deposits that are generally 1-3% of the property's purchase price. You can get this money back within a certain amount of time, depending upon the contract negotiated.

Your Offer is Accepted—Now What?

First, you need to get your initial paperwork signed and put down the initial deposit with your earnest and option money. This part of the process can be tricky since you have certain deadlines to follow. You will be given a certain period of time to inspect the property and decide whether you want it or not without losing your deposit. It's best to call all of your inspectors and contractors immediately to check the property and see what repairs it may need, if there are any issues with the foundation, if it has termites or whether those cracks in the wall are really just cosmetic. After this process, you can go back to the seller, request any relevant credits and renegotiate.

It's very important not to cut corners here. If it costs an extra $150 to check the pool, pay it. I heard a story recently about an investor who didn't do this and ended up paying $16,000 afterwards to fix the pool.

Of course, if you have a realtor, they can handle all of this with you. No one will be as invested as you are, however, so check in with your realtor every step of the way. If you're working without a realtor, don't forget to have an escrow company involved to protect your money and an attorney to double check your paperwork. And remember to check for liens!

The contract is contingent upon the inspection being completed. Once the contract no longer has any contingencies, you're responsible for your own payment on the property. At this point, you could potentially lose your deposit if you pull out of the deal.

When an offer is labeled as **contingent**, it means that the deal has been accepted pending certain additional conditions. Before the deal can be official and complete, those additional conditions must be met.

There are also other contingencies besides the inspection that you can place on a property when you make an offer. Often, people need to sell one house before they can afford to buy another; this contingency states that you want the property and will purchase on the condition that you sell the other one.

Contingencies can be helpful, but generally, the seller will include a contractual provision that states they can sell to someone else if that person is immediately ready to buy without contingencies. Whenever possible, it's best to be ready to make the deal without contingencies that can cause you to lose the property. If the buyer needs to sell sooner rather than later, you can potentially get a discount on the price if you're ready to buy immediately.

Working with a Lender

We've reviewed the need to shop around for lenders to get different rates. When you first put in an offer on a property, you'll need to show a proof of funds—also known as a pre-qualification letter. You aren't legally bound to the lender who writes this letter, so you can still shop around for a better rate. If you decide to purchase in cash, of course, you won't need a lender at all. With interest rates at an all-time low, however, I recommend borrowing the inexpensive money available.

When you get an estimated monthly payment amount, you can choose to include PITI–or Principal, Interest, Taxes and Insurance. There's no way to get out of paying property taxes and insurance, so including these amounts in your monthly mortgage payment makes it easier for you to budget.

When you fill out the contract, calculate how much money you're going to put down on the property so that the lender can accommodate the type of loan you want.

FHA Loan Offered by the Federal Home Administration

This loan is a fantastic way to buy your first property with a 3.5% down payment. You can get multiple FHA loans in your lifetime, but while you don't need to be a first-time homebuyer to qualify, you can only have one

FHA loan at a time. This prevents potential borrowers from using the loan program to buy investment properties.

With any other kind of loan where you put down less than 10%, the lender requires Purchase Mortgage Insurance (PMI). FHA mortgage loans don't require PMI, but they do require an Upfront Mortgage Insurance Premium (UFMIP) and a Mortgage Insurance Premium (MIP) to be paid instead. Depending on the terms and conditions of your home loan, most FHA loans today will require MIP for either 11 years or the lifetime of the mortgage.

Once you have 20% equity on the property, you can drop the extra insurance. Many borrowers think the PMI fee is too costly, but the PMI premium rate is 0.58-1.86% of the original amount of your loan. Freddie Mac estimates that most borrowers will pay only $30-$70 per month in PMI premiums for every $100,000 borrowed.

10% Down: The Vacation Home or First-Time Buyer

This loan amount is frequently used for a second home and provides a lower interest rate. For borrowers in the United States, the vacation home must typically be located at least 50 miles away from the primary residence in order to enjoy the second home classification and a lower interest rate. (Note that these laws are for the USA only.)

First-time buyers can often secure a lower down

payment as well. For a primary residence, the company you work for will sometimes offer loans at competitive rates to support you in purchasing your first home. Be sure to find out if your company offers this benefit.

20-25% Down

Many lenders require this amount at a minimum to get lower interest rates, and 20% will cost you more than if you put down 25%. You can also pay down the loan by paying points, but this only works if you plan to hold the property for a while. Remember that each point equates to 1% of your purchase price. Likewise, your interest rate can move from 5- to 4% on the entire loan by paying one percentage point. On a $100,000 purchase price, 1% would be $1,000. To determine whether you want to pay the $1,000, figure out how long it will take you to make it back. You can do this by comparing the 5% loan amount versus the 4% loan amount. So, if your monthly payment goes from $1,200 to $1,100, in one year, you will have broken even. After that, you'll save $100 a month—or $1,200 a year. Your credit score will also play a part in determining your interest rate.

The 2021 loan limit on conforming loans is $548,250 in most areas and $822,375 in high-cost areas. (A conforming loan is a mortgage with terms and conditions that meet the funding criteria of Fannie Mae and Freddie Mac, which, again, are backed by the government.) This means if you're borrowing more than that amount, it's considered a jumbo loan and your interest rate will be higher.

More Advantages with Lending

At the time of this writing, you can own up to 10 properties with one to four units in your own name using 30-year Fannie Mae and Freddie Mac loans. Many investing couples buy 10 in each of their names so that they can get a total of 20 together.

Preparing to Close

As soon as you're under contract, start preparing for anything you need in order to make the deal work. Find your contractors, get your property insurance and set up your electric, gas and water for after your closing dates. Your tenant may pay for utilities, but you need to have them in your name as soon as the title changes. It's a good idea to get the utility company information from the previous owner, or your realtor should be able to acquire the information easily.

You may also want to have a property manager in place or start running ads to find a tenant if you're managing the property yourself. Also, have a handyman or locksmith ready to change the locks on the property as soon as you close.

If you're borrowing with a traditional bank, it can take 30-45 days to get through closing. If you're purchasing on your own without a realtor, you can offer a 10, 20, 30 or 45-day period until closing. It isn't realistic to offer a 10-day close for a cash deal, however, as they usually close very quickly. Wholesale deals are generally in cash, so the sales can close as fast as within two days. These deals carry more risk, however, as you won't have time to conduct a thorough inspection in such a short timeframe.

It can feel daunting to close a transaction, especially when the paperwork seems to be the size of Mount Everest! Even so, every document has a reason to exist and needs your signature. To ease the stress, have your realtor or lending officer nearby to ensure you can get an explanation of what you're signing. Signatures are powerful and are upheld by the law, so you don't want to sign anything without understanding what it means. Fortunately, you do have a three-day grace period after signing to cancel the contract. The idea behind this is to ensure that no one is coerced into a decision. Most of the time, if you've made it to the signing table, you aren't planning to back out.

Closing and More About Escrow

Remember that escrow money is held with a third party to protect both the buyer and the seller. Often, it's a title company that offers the escrow services, and the seller will frequently recommend one. You will never pay or deposit money directly to the seller. The option money is generally wired to the third-party escrow account in addition to the funds due at closing. Only once all of the documents are signed by both parties will the funds be wired to the seller.

The title company insures the property's title with policies to the buyer and the lender to protect against any problems with the property or title. The escrow office is the neutral operator that handles all of the transactions between the parties. It ensures that all documents are signed and offers protection from someone running off with the funds.

It can cost $6,000 (sometimes more) for escrow, title and closing. Sometimes, it's more because property taxes or HOA fees are required to be paid up front. There's also a possibility of a "double close" if you purchase with a wholesaler—these are two separate transactions between the wholesaler and seller, and then between the wholesaler and buyer. (This isn't an ideal situation unless the price is truly right.)

Once both parties have signed the purchasing agreement, escrow is open so that the money can be transferred between parties.

Each expense is itemized on a closing document, so look through the document to see what you're being charged. You can also ask the escrow officer for an explanation or talk to your realtor about the closing costs. Remember that throughout the process, contingencies have deadlines. Again, if you miss the deadline to get out of your contract after the expectation window closes, you can lose your deposit.

You will need to sign the closing documents in the presence of a notary, and they will usually come to your house. Whenever you consider selling a property, the closing costs and realtor fees need to be included. The seller always pays both the buyer's and seller's agents, so when selling, you will be responsible for these costs. You should calculate 6% for the agents and about $6,000 for closing, including origination, title and other fees.

Whose Name Should Go On the Title?

This is one of the most important sections in this book! It's a *big* deal whose name is on the title and the grant deed of the property. Even if you're married and don't put your name on the title, you can be denied rights to the property unless you're in a state that declares what both parties own in a marriage as community property. In the event of death or divorce, this can be very tricky, so never waive your right to be legally bound to ownership.

Often, properties are held in the name of the individuals who own them. After you have a few assets and something to lose if you get sued, you'll want to shelter yourself from liability. As I mentioned early in the book, if you hold the title inside an LLC, you can only be sued for whatever is in that LLC and not for your personal assets. For this reason, people who own a lot of assets put properties into LLC entities.

Another way you can hold the property is in a trust. The reason to have a trust is that if you pass away, there's a contract to let the government know the name of the person you want to inherit your properties. This is one of the many advantages in real estate. You can arrange your investments in a way that you and your heirs never have to pay taxes on the properties through the 1031 exchange.

Before I explain further, I want to remind you again that I'm not a CPA or attorney. Make sure to consult with one on the recommendations to follow. I have consulted with several, and these are the best solutions I've found.

Most lenders can only lend to an individual for one-to-four-unit properties. The loan must stay in your personal name until closing. Afterwards, move your assets into the LLC (as long as the owners are members of it). After the asset is set up in an LLC, it needs to be assigned to your living trust in order to avoid probate.

When setting up your accounting, every property or few properties should hold title in the name of an LLC as a way to protect those assets and protect you personally from lawsuits. The fun part is that you get to name the LLC. For your personal property, you would put the title into the name of your trust. You can download the information from the Secretary of State website in the state where you're purchasing. Hiring an attorney to handle this for you will cost you double and isn't necessary. You can also use services like corporatecreations.com as well.

A registered agent is required in the state where you set up your LLC. Essentially, a registered agent is a place that accepts your mail. If you use your own address in the state where you live, it will be on public record. For $40 a year, you can maintain your privacy and be alerted anytime someone sends mail regarding your property. If you own a property in Texas and set up the LLC in Wyoming, for example, you will need a registered agent in Wyoming. Make sure that you go by the law and follow all of the rules to avoid penalties. Each state has different provisions and may have fees and annual reports required annually.

For example, there's a tax of $800 to have an LLC in the State of California. If I have a property set up in Wyoming, I still need to pay the $800 because I'm technically earning money in the state of California. When investors accumulate hundreds of properties, they start putting five to 10 properties together in each LLC.

Even though you can't move your property into an LLC until after you close with a Fannie Mae or Freddie Mac loan, you can still set up the LLC and have the bank account for the LLC open and ready for when your paperwork is completed.

The 1031 Exchange

The 1031 exchange enables you to defer paying taxes on a property for generations. It's the process of selling a property of equal or greater value within 180 days. The property exchange must be of like-kind and for business or investment use. You can exchange for lesser value, but you will need to pay tax on the amount of profit that doesn't transfer into the 1031 exchange.

You must complete your 1031 exchange within 180 days of selling your old property by purchasing one or more of the properties on a list you have identified for purchase. You can't buy property as part of the exchange that is not on the 45-day identification list, which must be accounted for with a qualified intermediary (often referred to as a QI).

The QI must remain arms-length from the transaction. In other words, they can have no existing relationship or interest in the asset. The QI prepares the legal agreements to properly structure the exchange. They will hold and safeguard your money from the sale of your property until you close on the replacement and ensure the replacement complies with IRS rules. You need to make sure you don't skip any deadlines or steps in the process, or your 1031 exchange can be disqualified. The exchange enables you to defer paying any tax on the property while you are alive. If you leave your properties to your kids in your trust, they utilize the step up in basis and can collect the asset upon your death tax-free. The reason to do a 1031 exchange is to maximize your ability to scale. If you have a lot of equity in a property, you can use that to buy more units or a more profitable deal while deferring all the taxes owed on the gains.

Closing in on the Finish Line

Once you get an offer accepted and the property passes your inspections, you're close to owning the property! This can bring a few fears to the surface. You may be responsible for tenants and payments on the loan to a bank. You are also trusting that your research, preparation and analysis of the numbers, location and strategy are going to work for you.

Take a deep breath! You're expanding your capacity for wealth and opportunity. It simply can't be done without any risk or having to deal with other people, including tenants and repair contractors.

But hey, if the numbers don't look right, or you start to see some red flags with the property, bail out. Even if you lose a few thousand dollars, it will be worth it.

If there are no red flags, however, your mindset can make a big difference in how the transaction plays out. Anytime you're in uncharted territory, you're probably going to have nervous moments. Even Tony Robbins says you never fully get rid of fear, you just walk through it as it comes. Inevitably, once you're on the other side, you can say you made it!

Sometimes, I look back on things I've accomplished, and my stomach still aches with pangs of fear I went through at the time. Once I was through it, however, it wasn't nearly as scary. If you aren't willing to take these steps, you'll never make it to millionaire status. You must learn to live with uncertainty.

Now that you're on the purchasing train, you need to know how to find tenants and keep them paying, which we'll cover in detail in the next chapter.

Home Warranties

It's fairly standard when purchasing a home through the MLS to have the seller pay for a home warranty. Of course, like with all insurance, companies like to pay out as little as possible.

Home warranties can be handy, but these days, I find them to be more trouble than they're worth. You generally pay $75 for a service call, and they always make you wait a long time for approval. At one point, I had a bad leak in a home and just bypassed the company, paying to fix the leak out of pocket.

The vendors that work with insurance companies are also not the best. The home warranty companies pay very discounted rates, so any vendor who signs up with them isn't making much—certainly not fair market rates. This frequently affects the quality of the work they do, although I've had a few successful transactions over the years. I wouldn't turn down a free policy if I were you, but don't expect that it will mean no hassles or no additional expenses for repairs.

Exit Strategies: When to Hold and When to Sell

An exit strategy is simply a plan you can pivot into if the first one doesn't work, or if an opportunity to scale up once profit has been made on your investment comes along. If you aren't making enough money from a long-term rental, it could mean looking at turning the property into a short-term rental so you can collect more money. You could also sell the property, take your profits and move on to the next.

Refinance and HELOCs

A refinance and HELOC (Home Equity Line of Credit) are two more ways to leverage effectively and get more money out of an asset without selling it. Decide on your objective for getting access to the extra cash. If it's for something short term, the HELOC is a great option. You can take advantage of all-time low interest rates and only pay back what you borrow. You also don't need to pay refinancing fees, which is good, because refinancing costs as much as closing on a new property. With a HELOC, you're creating a new loan with a new rate and terms.

A great reason to refinance is to lower your interest rate or to get the cash (equity) out of your property. With a cash out refinance, you don't need to pay for any of the appreciation you take out (although upon sale, you will need to calculate the entire profit on a property). If you're buying another property with the money long-term or if interest rates are decreasing so that you can take advantage of better loan terms, it can be a good choice.

Tax Advantages and Expenses

There are tax implications for holding a property for less than one year and not living in the property for two of the last five years. Ideally, you want to hold a property for at least one year to avoid short-term capital gains taxes, which can be as high as 37%.

Additionally, one of the best tax strategies out there is to live in a property for two out of the last five years as your primary residence—doing so can get you $250,000 as a single person or $500,000 as a couple tax-free. If you aren't opposed to moving every few years, this is a fantastic benefit.

You should always consider the value of holding an asset versus selling and moving on to a different strategy. Of course, you can simply hold on to every asset and keep buying more properties, as there's a lot of financial security in holding assets over time. Your rents continue to increase, and so do the property values.

While a flip can make you a quick and impressive cash return, it doesn't take full advantage of holding an asset. Many investors choose to sell once a property appreciates and move into something larger using a 1031 exchange. You need to calculate the cost of the sale, but other than that, the tax advantage is almost unbeatable. To learn more about this topic, check out *The Book on Tax Strategies for the Savvy Real Estate Investor* by Matt MacFarland and Amanda Han.

How Do You Get the Best Return?

Getting the best return is always a bit of a juggling game. There are people who sold properties three years ago in Austin, where I live, and now wish they had kept them. They took their profits to buy something else, but likely would have made more if they held the properties for longer.

Once a property appreciates 25%, many believe that's a good time to buy a bigger property. You can always buy and hold for a few years and go into a 1031 exchange or pay taxes. Even simply buying and holding properties is a winning proposition. Almost every option in real estate is a road to save on taxes and make more profit.

Chapter 7 Actions:

1. Get organized! Collect all of your paperwork and documents and develop a system to track all the details of your eventual property portfolio.

2. Set up your LLC and/or review a plan for holding your property.

3. Make a checklist of all the steps you need to take before making an offer on a property. Work with your experienced team to research liens and to review inspections and important deadlines. Make a loan checklist that includes a term duration (30-year fixed is best), hidden fees, all inspections (pest, septic, pool and foundation), insurance, contingencies and closing dates.

4. Determine your teams—those you must rely on a pre-offer and mid-offer as well as during acceptance review, closing and escrow.

5. What is your ideal deal and offer? What are the projected returns?

EIGHT

THE INS AND OUTS OF PROPERTY MANAGEMENT

> ❝ *I just want women to always feel in control.*
> *Because we're capable. We're so capable.*
> —Nicki Minaj

We truly are so capable. But I didn't hear those words often while I was growing up. I knew I could survive, but I heard the way to do that was to get a job, pay the bills and do it all yourself. I actually thought I had to do it all myself or people would take advantage of me, causing me to lose everything I worked hard to create. I wanted to prove to myself that I could do it alone and believed that if I needed support, it was because I wasn't smart enough to figure it all out myself.

As a result, I was overwhelmed because it was so much for me to manage on my own. I managed 20 units by myself at one point because I wanted to save money and be in control, but this limited me. I was constantly putting out fires that could have been handled by someone else while I looked for new properties. I was keeping myself in handcuffs.

In this chapter, I make arguments for both self-managing your properties and hiring a property manager. My bottom line is that regardless of what you determine is right for you, always measure your time in dollars to see if it makes sense. Make sure that you trust there are others who can support and help you and that you aren't doing all of it alone.

One of the biggest factors that hold people back in buying real estate is the idea that they will get calls at all hours to fix toilets. Well, that can be true! It isn't the case most of the time, though. Even if you're managing your own property, you will still have a handyman, plumber and electrician. Plus, emergencies are rare.

Should You Hire a Property Manager?

If you're debating whether or not to hire a property manager, the first thing to consider is whether you live close to the property. If you're far away or even in another state, it generally makes sense to hire a professional to take care of the tenants. On the other hand, I have friends who live in LA and own long-term rentals in Hawaii that they self-manage. They choose to fly out, find their own tenants and manage the places on their own; as a result, they get an all-expenses-paid, tax-deductible trip to Hawaii. For them, it's worth it. At present, the tax laws state that you need to conduct more than half of your trip as business in order to write it off.

One of the most difficult parts of management is finding a good tenant. I can't emphasize this enough. Tenants can make or break you. They're the ones paying your bills, so if they aren't responsible and reliable, no management company is going to be able to do a good job for you.

Many people think hiring a property manager will guarantee that everything runs smoothly, but my worst experience with a tenant happened even though they were approved by my property manager. Still, many property managers are seasoned and follow a strict protocol.

Another big factor is the cost of paying for a manager. They charge anywhere from 25-100% of the first month's rent to place a tenant. Then, they charge 6-10% of the monthly rent to manage the property. It's possible to get a better deal, but you want someone who is thorough. Some property managers also charge a premium for repairs, so if the plumber charges $200, the property manager bills you $225. These fees can be steep and cut into your profit margins, and they need to be calculated into the cost of the rental.

After years of managing my own properties, I've found that it's well worth it to hire a manager. Take the time to find the right one, and ask the right questions to discern the exact amount of fees you'll be paying. Don't be afraid to be specific about what you need. If you aren't sure, hire someone you feel is honest, takes their work and reputation seriously, has the experience you need and charges fairly. You can save money if you hire someone with less experience, but you'll likely need to manage them a bit more.

I used to feel bad asking detailed questions of potential property managers. I felt that questioning their methods was disrespectful of their expertise and process. Then, I hired a property manager who didn't vet a tenant properly and realized that I was the one responsible for paying the bills when the tenant didn't pay rent.

There's a way to take ownership and lead without overstepping your bounds. As your portfolio builds, so will your team, and you will need to get comfortable steering the ship if you want your investments to be profitable.

Large property management companies are well-seasoned and have systems in place, but if they expand too quickly, there are going to be details that fall through the cracks. The company that didn't find me a good tenant didn't meet the people in person first. They based it entirely on the application qualifications. They said they were concerned the person would accuse them of discrimination if they met them and didn't rent to them. While housing discrimination is very real and systemic, in this scenario, it was a far-fetched excuse for bad management.

I *always* like to meet potential tenants and feel strongly that every property manager should as well.

I also only realized the tenants had stopped paying rent when I saw there were no funds posted to my account. When I finally questioned the managers, I realized for the first time that they knew very little about the tenant. Given the circumstances, it didn't appear that they checked the application well, either. It's critical that your property manager takes the time to properly check tenants' credit reports, references and application validity (yes, there are people who lie on their applications!). Never hesitate to monitor your manager—after all, they work for you!

Make sure that your property manager goes by the property regularly and stays on top of payments. They should know how to communicate and connect with tenants, too. If tenants don't feel like repairs are being made in a timely manner or that no one is holding them accountable to keep the place in good order, it will be easy for them to take advantage of the property.

Property Manager Responsibilities

Whether you're managing a property yourself or hiring a manager to handle it, it is a responsibility that should be taken seriously. In addition to finding a tenant, property managers handle:

- Rent increases.
- Evictions when you need to get someone out.
- Repairs—they will call you if a repair is more than $200, but otherwise, they'll just get the job done and bill you.
- Maintenance—good managers do inspections outside and inside the property periodically to ensure tenants are taking care of your asset.
- Conflicts between units when tenants don't get along with each other.
- Accounting—there's generally a portal where you can see all your income and expenses; they can also send profit and loss statements and will give you a 1099 and full accounting at the end of the year so you can file your taxes.

You Don't Always Get What You Pay For

There's an old saying that you get what you pay for, but I've paid a lot and gotten mediocre results. I've also paid a little and gotten great results. It depends on what you need done and how much it's worth to you in money and time. It's also important to trust your inner voice that feels confident in the person you are hiring regardless of the price.

Here are a few examples. When I self-managed, I needed a new washer-dryer for a unit. I checked the prices at three stores. I had a few options and was in the process of making my decision, but I got so wrapped up in getting the best one at the best price that I spent hours on it. I even called a friend to ask her what she thought. "Time is money," she responded, "so at the end of the day, it doesn't matter. If you pay a few hundred dollars more, it still doesn't matter as long as you get it off your plate quickly." She was right. Paying someone $50 to take care of it for me would have been worth it.

Another time, I hired a property manager for 6% per month, and I was thrilled because it was well below the usual 8-10%. Not only did they find me the worst tenant I have ever had, but they also didn't monitor their staff enough to ensure that my eviction paperwork was done correctly. They rarely returned my calls quickly but always charged my 6% like clockwork. I ended up getting rid of them and hiring a company for 10%. They were local to the area the property was in and raised the rent from $1,225 to $1,425. It was easy for them to do local checkups on the property, and their vetting process was more thorough than the 6% company. Have you done the easy math here? The $200 extra per month more than paid for the new management.

The Benefits and Downsides of Self-Managing

I managed my own properties for 20 years. By doing so, I saved money on having to pay someone else to do it, learned how to do the job and had ultimate control. If you don't have any issues with the scope of the work, the most important skill to master is finding a tenant. Once you've done that job yourself, it's easier to understand what skills you might want from a manager in the future.

If you're self-managing, make sure that you don't get too chummy with the tenants. If they know you're the owner, for example, they'll automatically assume you have a lot of money and may ask for a lot more than they would from a manager. Owning properties is a business, and I find that ultimately, it's better for tenants to remain tenants, not friends.

I don't recommend renting to friends unless you don't care about the amount of money you get for rent. It's difficult to ask friends to pay for damages or to be stern with them if the rent is late. I prefer to keep my properties and my friends separate. This may sound harsh, but imagine having to raise rent on your friends. If you ever need to enforce a rule, it's important to keep your boundaries clear and your relationships professional.

Criteria for Placing a Tenant

Check credit scores, employment, previous residency, criminal background, income and savings accounts. These factors will give you a good sense of whether the tenants pay on time and have a good track record of paying bills. Always double-check references! This is a great way to ensure your potential tenant will be responsible for keeping your property well-maintained and that they will pay in a timely manner.

You can check credit scores on creditkarma.com for free. The prospective tenant will need to create an account and send you the results. You can also request their credit scores from Experian, Transunion and Equifax—the three major creditors. There are services that run credit checks as well.

Look for a credit score of over 700. Time and time again, this is a good indicator showing that people pay their bills and prioritize their finances; however, if you're renting to people with lower incomes or in an area where more people have financial challenges, you may not be able to get a score of 700 or more. In those cases, be sure to verify employment and other information.

Fees You May Want to Charge

You can charge $35-$65 per application if you find that vetting a tenant is a lot of work, or if you have to hire an assistant to handle the workflow. Even if you are doing the work, I feel this fee is justified. Property managers almost always charge this fee, but as a mom and pop manager, I rarely did.

Most mom and pop landlords also don't realize that you can charge a fee of $25-$50 monthly per pet. This is in addition to a $500-$1,000 security deposit or a non-refundable deposit that's often paid up front. Pets have the potential to cause damage to properties. They scratch floors and pee in homes and apartments. They also leave excessive hair that's difficult to clean. I love dogs and cats and accept them in all of my properties, but I do charge a fee.

Quarterly Visits and Inspections

Before I ran into some real professionals in property management, I rarely visited my properties. Now, I walk through the inside and outside of every property every three to six months, which is invaluable. Your tenants will know you're watching what they're doing and that you will hold them accountable.

These walk-throughs also let you see things the tenants may not notice that are in need of repair, and it gives you the opportunity to show you care. You can ask the tenants if they have any needs that aren't being met with the property. You may notice the grass is dead, and they'll tell you, "Oh, yeah, the sprinklers stopped coming on three weeks ago!" (That has happened to me more than once.) Carry a clipboard with you so that you can go through each room and ensure everything is in working order.

What Do You Charge for Rent?

This question is very important. If you charge too much, no one will look at the place. If you charge too little, you'll kick yourself for leaving money on the table. Luckily, we live in a time when it's fairly easy to research what to charge for rents. If you buy a property through a realtor, I'm sure they would be happy to check for you or refer you to a property manager who may give you advice. You can check Zillow and Craigslist to get an idea of what rents are going for or use rentometer.com.

When there's a housing shortage and high demand, you may want to start pricing a bit higher and see if you get any calls. Otherwise, you can lower the price. I recommend waiting a few days before lowering it, however. In the past, I would get nervous and impatient and lower the rent too soon. At the end of the day, if you're in an area where people want to live, you will find good tenants.

It's always scary when you buy a new property or haven't rented one yet. I've had clients tell me they prefer to have tenants already in place so that they don't need to look for any. The trouble with that is you're inheriting people you didn't vet yourself. While it's an extra step, selecting my own tenants is always my preference.

Airbnb and Long-Term Furnished Rentals

Airbnb and the furnished property takes some time to get used to because at first glance, it seems like it will be a lot of work. Once you start to see the numbers and make back the money for the furniture expenses however, you'll start to enjoy this model. It's a lot of work up front, but it gets more streamlined after guests start booking regularly.

There are variables to consider if you choose to commit to short-term rentals, however. You need to feel confident that you're in an area where people want to rent at a premium for a furnished rental. With a long-term rental—where you have someone like a traveling nurse staying in your place—you can get a premium in price and will have very little to maintain.

Of course, you can always hire a property manager to manage the bookings and maintenance, though they usually take 10-25%. Remember to always check regulations and make sure the numbers work to convert to a long-term lease if the regulations on short-term rentals in the area change.

Leasing Agreement and Terms

A key way to protect yourself and your assets is to create a detailed lease agreement. If you state all of the terms clearly in the lease that your tenant signs, you'll be able to take action if the rules are broken. You can download a standard lease agreement from the internet for free (I like turbotenant.com for a small fee) and hire an attorney to check one for you for a low rate. I don't think you need an attorney to look it over, however. Just make sure that any provision or rules you want to include in the lease are noted. I often have tenants sign an addendum for rules like "water the grass" as well.

You want to make sure you include details specific to your preference in the lease, such as no pets and no subleasing. I've had properties where tenants decided to pay me and rent the rooms out to people I didn't know. A big business for some entrepreneurial types is to pay the rent for a few years and then sublet the unit to Airbnb. This is known as arbitrage, and these terms can be openly negotiated between a renter and owner. If you don't want to offer this option, make sure it's written in the lease. This is another reason to have a manager or to check the property yourself quarterly.

You can set whatever terms you want for the lease duration, though a 12-month lease term is fairly standard. After that, you can require an additional one-year lease term to be signed again or move on to month-by-month. Rent increases generally happen once a year, but if a tenant signs on for two years, they lock in the rent rate for the duration of the lease period. You can also do shorter term leases, but the wear and tear of switching tenants so frequently doesn't make it worthwhile unless you're renting the place with furniture. If the property has furniture, there won't be a bunch of dents in the walls from moving items in and out or putting pictures on the walls.

Tenants should pay rent on the first of every month. Some landlords will allow a few days' grace period, while others charge late fees. The charge and terms for late fees needs to be written in the lease.

Make sure you have a clear and easy system for tenants to pay their rent. I use Venmo and automatic deposit. My property managers usually have their own systems to collect payments and then automatically deposit the rents in my account every month.

If you do need to take action against a tenant, make sure you know the laws in your state. There are "tenant-friendly" and "landlord-friendly" states and cities. Removing a tenant in California or New York City is infinitely more challenging than doing so in Texas. If you're owed money by a tenant, I always recommend small claims court, because you won't need to pay for an attorney. You'll need the address of the tenants in order to serve them your filing. If they've moved and you can't find them, it will be difficult to collect your money.

I can't emphasize enough the importance of a signature. The lease signed by both tenant and landlord is binding in court and will protect both parties, but it is especially helpful for protecting your rights to your assets.

Make sure you keep all of your signed documents in a safe place and keep them appropriately updated. It's also a good idea to require renters to carry insurance. If there's a robbery or a fire, their personal belongings will only be covered by their own coverage. Again, put this requirement in the lease so that in the unfortunate circumstance something happens, you won't be responsible.

Rent Increases

Mom and pop property owners who manage on their own often don't raise rents. They're happy if the tenant pays consistently and doesn't call them with any complaints. They also tend to be more connected to the tenants because they handle all of the interactions. Because of that, they may know the tenant's son just left for college and that money is tight. The landlords then feel greedy or ungrateful for raising rents. This is one reason why investors like property managers. The owner is then removed from any emotional connection that may make it harder to handle the business part of the transaction, which is the main reason you own property in the first place.

Sometimes, however, it isn't a bad idea to refrain from raising rents on good tenants. You may be happy with the amount of rent you are receiving and value a great tenant. You may know they are on a fixed budget and want to support them by stabilizing rent. It gets tricky when you live in a rent-controlled city like Los Angeles, where the rent increases are mandated by the city.

If you can only raise rents 3-5% per year and you miss

a few years, you'll never be able to make up the loss with the tenant. This can turn into a problem if you want to sell the property, because the value is less when you can only collect a small amount of rent and can't easily remove a tenant. In a landlord-friendly city, you can raise the rent to the market price anytime, but if the rent is very low and protected by rental law enforced by the state, tenants won't easily move out. You can Google the laws for tenants in each state. As I mentioned earlier, these factors should weigh into your decision about where to buy properties.

Evictions

When tenants don't pay their rent or violate the rules outlined in the lease, you have the right to evict them. You should always attempt to work with them first, however. If they haven't paid rent, find out why and when they will pay it.

During the COVID-19 pandemic, many areas had a moratorium on evictions. This meant that landlords couldn't evict tenants for nonpayment until the end of the moratorium. The laws under COVID-19 also stipulated a forbearance on mortgages. This meant you could ask the lender to let you hold off on mortgage payments without penalty. This provision was great for people who truly couldn't make the payments, but forbearance still goes on your record and can affect your ability to get more loans in the near future. At the time of writing this book, the moratorium and forbearance laws are still in effect in many states. California will have restricted rent increases for close to three years under the current laws enacted during the pandemic.

The laws for eviction and the process you have to go through vary depending on location, but in general (when not under COVID-19 guidelines), these are the reasons you can ask someone to leave:

- Violation of lease agreement
- Unpaid rent
- Illegal activity
- Health and safety violations
- Threats or unsafe behavior
- Providing false information on the lease application
- Breaking HOA rules
- Excessive noise

At the point you file with the court for an eviction, it's reasonable to assume that you've asked the tenants to comply with the terms of the lease agreement and that they've refused or ignored your requests. Always give the tenant a few days to correct the issue after your request, but if no change has occurred, you'll have no choice but to file with the court.

Eviction is a last resort, but it's the only way to remove a tenant once you've tried all avenues of communication.

With an eviction, there's a risk that the tenants will destroy the property because they're angry about being displaced. It's also costly to switch out tenants because there's generally cleaning and painting to be done and perhaps more to fix. The tenant can also drag their heels once the notice is served and refuse to leave until the final court order, which can take months. While you're waiting to go to court regarding an eviction, you can accept no money from the tenant. As soon as you do, the court considers you willing to accept partial payments. This is another reason why landlord-friendly states make it easier to conduct business.

When you start the process, you need to post a notice on the tenant's door to pay within three days. The tenant usually has 30 days to vacate from that point unless you take it to court. After you get the judgment in court, the tenant has five days to appeal.

Remember that until the judgment is final and an officer is sent to your property to get the tenant out, you will receive no income. These are the reasons why eviction is a last resort and in many ways, a landlord's nightmare. But as with all business struggles, you get through it. My last eviction was in Texas and went rather smoothly. The tenants got the notice and moved out within the 30 days during COVID-19. I did lose a few months' rent, but they left promptly.

There have been ways to apply for Federal Rental Assistance if the tenants couldn't pay during COVID-19.

Since my tenants decided to leave without a discussion, I was happy to find a new tenant and move on. In your budget, this would be a line item called vacancy. It's wise to budget 5% monthly for possible vacancies because even if you don't have an eviction, you may have some down-time when transitioning between tenants.

Reserves and Expenses

As we're reviewing some of the downsides of managing tenants, you're likely seeing more reasons to keep reserve funds in your bank account. In addition to possible vacancies at 5%, an additional 10% of the rent each month should go to savings for standard monthly operational expenses including:

- Property tax (interest is tax deductible)
- Insurance
- Gardeners and pest control
- Water and utilities (if they aren't covered by the tenant)

Then there's capital expenditures. These are larger costs like electrical, plumbing, roof and HVAC. Also, the expenses for transitions between tenants for wear and tear which can't be covered by the new tenant must be budgeted for. The plan is to make more than you spend, so with real estate, you will frequently move money in and out of your account due to all of the activity.

Security Deposit

The security deposit you charge your tenants will give you some protection against property damage and unpaid rent. You can generally charge up to two months' rent as security. The amount should be held in a separate account, and depending on the state, you may owe interest to the tenant on that deposit annually. Not every tenant will ask for interest, and it's generally a nominal fee. So you don't need to worry about any recourse from it. If a pet is involved, you may want to charge an additional pet deposit or take a non-refundable deposit. As long as it isn't a service pet, you can charge either or both of those fees. You can request that your unit not be rented to pets as well, although you'll have a smaller pool of candidates.

A new company called Rhino emerged a few years ago that gives you insurance for a monthly fee to cover your security deposits. You can also get a "double rhino" if you want extra coverage for your tenants.

When the tenants move out, you can do a walk-through so that they know what you expect to be fixed. The property or unit should look in the same condition as when they received it except for normal wear and tear. The money that can be kept from a security deposit will depend on how many years the tenants have occupied the unit. You can deduct a portion for painting and floors. At times you can also deduct a fee for any cleaning required beyond normal wear and tear.

Tenants may request a walk-through of the unit after departing. My recommendation is not to do the walk-through with the tenant present if you're self-managing the property, because they tend to pressure you into getting the deposit back right away. Over the years while self-managing, I've found that when I walk through with tenants, they don't like hearing about money taken from their deposit for repairs. It's easier to let them leave and then inspect it once they're gone. Depending upon the state, you have approximately 21-30 days to return the balance of the deposit to the tenants.

In the past, it was popular to also collect first and last months' rent. In certain states, taking the last month's rent is prohibited by law. I decided to stop this practice because I didn't like holding that much of my tenants' money. While this is designed to protect the landlord, I'd rather support others to have more choices to invest those funds. Tenants will sometime ask to have the security deposit used as their last month's rent. I always say no to this, because the deposit is the money used to make repairs, if necessary. My current policy is to collect one month's rent as the security deposit.

Chapter 8 Actions:

1. Carefully weight the pros and cons of self-managing your properties versus hiring a manager or management company. Determine whether you have the time and interest in handling the inevitable hassles.

2. If you have decided to hire a property manager, make a thorough checklist of your criteria and requirements.

NINE
CREATE TEAMS AND PARTNERSHIPS

> *I can do things you cannot. You can do things I cannot. Together, we can do great things.*
> —*Mother Teresa*

Of all of the chapters in this book, this one may be the most important. Relationships are everything. However big you decide to grow your real estate empire, you will inevitably need to deal with other people. The connections you make and the relationships you cultivate will always play a big factor in your success and affect how quickly you grow your wealth.

For so long, I thought the only person I could trust was myself. I did every task alone, which made everything more difficult. Today, I surround myself with a team, but I still have trouble delegating at times. If you're like me, I want you to know you aren't the only one, and it's okay to be a work in progress. Once you get your team in place, you will collect more profit than you would troubleshooting the small stuff, and you'll get better at delegating. Even if you're shy or uncomfortable in large groups, that isn't a good enough reason not to pursue your dreams.

The Realtor

Let's assume you're brand new to real estate or you own a few properties and want to buy more. The hardest part is the beginning. You're in the learning phase, building out your pipeline and connections to find opportunities.

You can use Zillow, realtor.com or another of the major real estate sites to find deals, but most of those will have already been picked over by other people. You can also find a wholesaler to connect you with off-market deals, or you can hire a realtor to look around for properties for you. If you're looking for properties in the same area, please be respectful of your realtor's time, however. While you don't have to sign an exclusive agreement with a realtor, you may want to if you connect with someone who understands investing. That way, they'll be committed to spending the extra time to support you. Just call them frequently to remind them you're still looking. Signed agreements are more common when you're listing a property for sale, however.

If you're looking in many different areas, you may

need a few agents who will send you properties to consider. Working with several agents is very common when you're seeking larger properties like multi-families or mobile home parks. The reason for this is that commercial realtors often cultivate relationships with property owners and get off-market deals. The more deals you can access, the more you can analyze and make offers. You may need to look at 100 properties to find one or two.

Here, I'm going to mention focus again—you will be most successful by focusing on one strategy and location in the beginning, and the more specific you get, the more a realtor can help you. Just like with a property manager, don't settle on the first realtor you meet. Interview a few and get to know how they work. How attentive are they? How many leads do they give you? How willing are they to answer your questions and drive around to look for properties? How knowledgeable are their answers?

Relationships can take time to cultivate, and finding the realtors who will get you from point A to B can take even longer. Don't fret. Everyone has to start somewhere, and spending your time cultivating these connections can be rewarding and fun.

The Lender

I've already included extensive information about loans, but it's important to understand the value your bank and lender will play in getting a deal done.

Most investments won't be paid in full with your money. Establishing solid relationships with lenders who can get you great rates and terms on loans will be critical to your success in real estate. Get to know the players at your local banks. Make connections with people who have a high net worth, as you may need them to come in as principal partners on deals for a small percentage. Remember that lending money to a reliable investor is a great way to get returns that can be anywhere from 8-12% annualized. I don't know any bank that pays that!

Another advantage to knowing your bankers is that local banks sometimes get foreclosure listings. If someone defaults on their loan, the banks will sell you the property at a discount to get it off their books.

In the 2008 crash, short sales became very popular. Remember that a short sale is when a bank allows a property to be sold at a discounted set price, which is agreed upon between the bank and the homeowner. (The difference between a short sale and foreclosure is that short sales are voluntary and require approval from the lender; foreclosures are involuntary, where the lender takes legal action to take control of and sell the property.) Due to the criteria set forth, it can take up to three months to negotiate agreed terms and close short sales.

I also recommend having more than one bank connection. I've had great relationships with certain lenders, but at certain points, the terms changed out of my favor. If the rate your preferred bank quotes you seems high, you'll want to shop around.

The level of service you get should also factor into your decision. I had a lender offer me a great rate on a property, but they called me two weeks later asking if I could push back the closing date by two weeks! The lag time in letting me know they wouldn't make my deadline could have lost me the deal. Luckily, I scrambled and found someone else who met my terms, deadline and service requirements.

As you develop these relationships, you'll know who to call based on the specifics of the deal and the variables involved. Your roster will become more valuable as your needs grow and change. There's just no question that it's faster and easier to get deals done when you have a pool of lenders to connect with.

The Contractor and Maintenance Workers

As I've said, one way to find properties at a discount is to be willing to do repairs on fixer uppers. Unless you're truly skilled at repairs, you will need to find a contractor and a team to do the work. You can mitigate some of the stress of managing the construction by hiring a General Contractor (GM). It will be their job to hire the team and manage them, and they will generally charge 10-20% over the budget for that service.

Even if you know and trust that you're getting the

work done, it's best to oversee the project or GM. At the end of the day, you're the one paying the bill, so you'll want to be certain the work is completed on time and to your specifications.

When gathering any members of a team, get referrals and a few estimates. Referrals aren't a guarantee that the work will go smoothly, though. I know someone who hired a contractor based on a friend's referral, and a lawsuit ensued because all the work was done incorrectly. Of course, that's a worst case scenario, but definitely be as thorough as possible before hiring someone.

What about the contractor's payment schedule? Let's say you're working on a rehab and flip. You might pay 20% of the supplies to start, and the contractor might need 10 or 20% to pay their crew (a lot of the time, contractors don't have extra cash flow). You can pay another 20% when they do the flooring, another 20% for paint, another 20% for electrical work and so on. Check at each point to make sure the appropriate portion of the job was completed to your satisfaction.

If you borrowed money from a private lender, expect a payment schedule at each phase. On a flip, you will need access to some cash reserves because you don't want to be slowed down by waiting for an inspection to release next payments.

Managing your own construction team is time-consuming because you'll need to keep the workers incentivized to stay on track. Some people don't want to deal with this sort of babysitting and monitoring, but you don't want a worker taking your money and taking off to another country (yes, this can happen!).

Once you have a team you trust, you can loosen the reins a bit and jobs can become much simpler. Since you likely won't have overseen any construction projects before, doing so may feel overwhelming. To help you get started, meet with other investors and get references until you find the right workers or a partner.

Strive to get the best out of people at the best price for the job. Don't be afraid to make a change, fire someone or let them know the relationship isn't working. Also, don't rush to pay the final balance—if a job hasn't been done to your specifications, stand your ground. Workers will generally get pushy once they've completed a job because they want to get paid. Be fair and ethical, but make sure the work was done correctly.

Once you start working on a project, ideas for more improvements will start flooding in. "Wouldn't it be nice to open up this room?" "The water heater will look better out of the house." "Let's paint the walls yellow." But after the initial estimate, these are "change orders." While they may be great ideas, they also may not be in your budget, so get an estimate before authorizing the extra work. I recently built a small deck on a property. The original idea was to raise it to the level of the house, but I opted to keep it closer to the ground to save a few thousand dollars.

You will need a handyman or woman to manage

smaller tasks. Unfortunately, these people charge up to $100 an hour to do maintenance work—and some charge those prices even though they aren't good at their job! It doesn't mean you won't be able to find good help at reasonable rates, but watch out for vendors who overcharge. For a handyman, I think $30-$50 an hour should be the top rate for someone very efficient who also has some plumbing and electrical knowledge. Again, get referrals— and don't pay for the job until it's completed. These days, you can use services like TaskRabbit, Angie's List, Yelp or NextDoor to quickly find someone with online reviews. Once you've rented your property, you still might need to find a gardener, a pest control company, a pool person and a cleaning crew.

If you rent to long-term tenants, you should have them pay for all of the standard maintenance items. That way, you won't need to manage anything yourself other than the mortgage payment and repairs. It's a great practice to set up a checklist so that you don't miss any details. You can download my free team building checklist at www. themillionairessmentality.com/teambuilding.

The Bookkeeper

With real estate, managing the financial details will help you stay profitable and moving towards your goals. You don't need to be a rock star with numbers, but you do need to keep track of your budget and expenses. Accounting will also make it a lot easier when it's tax time, especially as you implement more sophisticated strategies to make and save money.

My suggestion is to keep a separate checkbook and account for each property. If you use one account for all properties, you'll need to be much more careful with your records. Quicken, QuickBooks, Excel and Google Docs will all be helpful to you in maintaining your records.

You may want to hire a bookkeeper, which means you'll have to give them authority to see the numbers. For your protection and security, don't allow them to create transactions until you trust them completely. Then, monitor your books and P&L statements monthly to ensure their accuracy. I recommend automating any monthly bills like electric, cable or water. These small bills can take a lot of time to track, especially once you start growing your portfolio.

Questions to Ask When Hiring Your Team

These are the basic questions to ask anyone you are considering hiring to be a member of your team:

- Have you done this job before?
- Do you have references?
- Do you have samples of your work?
- What are your fees, and how do you expect to

be paid—all at once or on a payment schedule?

See how responsive they are to your phone messages and texts. Timeliness is an indication of how they're managing their business as well as the kind of customer service you'll receive. If you hire somebody and can't get in touch with them when there's an issue, that can be incredibly frustrating. To avoid those situations, you can sometimes work with vendors on a trial basis by giving them a small job before a large one. Once your systems are set up, it will be a lot easier to manage people, properties and projects.

Investing Partners

When I first started looking into partnerships or at investing in larger projects where I put money in deals without managing them myself, I was nervous. I felt like I was giving up control. But letting experienced investors work your money into a profitable deal is a great way to get into real estate investing.

With a property investment group, you become part of an LLC. You're one of many on the title, and you're putting your trust in someone else to handle all of the details and earn you a profit. While I still have a hard time giving up control, I've found that when you invest with specialists in multi-family, flips or storage units, you can find a team that knows their end of the business well. It isn't without risks, but they're mitigated risks.

No one wants to lose money or get into a bad deal, so learn to trust yourself. Celebrate your wins and learn from your setbacks. Working with others will ultimately be more rewarding and get you further a lot faster.

Whom Do You Trust?

The larger your portfolio, the larger your team will become. When your assets build, the good news is that you aren't only overseeing more people but also more money.

Remember my story about the financial advisor who sold me annuities I didn't need? He had lots of credentials, and he was a smart talker. I assumed he knew better, so I didn't trust myself. As a result, I missed out on about $80,000 in lost opportunities, fees and penalties. It was a lot of money, and I was furious. But today, I see that I made so much more after understanding his offerings as bad deals.

That experience also led me to create Wealth Building Concierge. I didn't want to see other women be led astray by fiduciaries who took advantage of their trust. I can't guarantee you'll never lose money or get into a bad deal, but I can tell you to do your due diligence. Once you've done that, real estate investing involves a certain amount of letting go. It's what is required to build the gains and wealth you want.

Real estate is still a male-dominated space, and some women in the business feel like men don't treat them equally. I have many male and female partners, and I believe it comes down to the person you're working with, regardless of gender. If you assume you have a right to be in the industry, you will command respect from most people. If someone doesn't treat you well, don't do business with them regardless of ethnicity, gender or reputation. Make it a rule to only choose partners you sincerely believe are good people.

Chapter 9 Actions:

1. Make a list of your current and potential team members. If you don't have connections now, how can you cultivate relationships that lead to a great support system? Be sure to have at least one back up for each.

- Lender
- Realtor(s)
- Property Manager
- Handyman
- Contractor(s)
- Subcontractors

2. For each team member, ask the following:

- Who are their references?

- What are their fees for every step of the job?
- How do they expect to be paid and how often?
- How much experience do they have?
- How well do they know the specific area where you're buying?
- How quickly do the prospects answer your messages?
- What other projects are they involved in?
- After your call, do they follow up with you or are they looking for an easy sell?

TEN
THE BIG MONEY FREEDOM STRETCH

> *Make the most of yourself by fanning the tiny, inner sparks of possibility into flames of achievement.*
> —*Golda Meir*

Once your ducks are in a row and you have a plan in place for growing your wealth through real estate, you can take what you learn and start investing. Now you understand that saving and budgeting and investing it in real estate can add up to a huge amount of money in the future. The actions you take today will lead to the free lifestyle and wealth that will prevent you from worrying about having too little money now or later.

Now that you realize you deserve money and it's possible for you to make a lot of it, there's no reason why you shouldn't get started. You just have to expand your mindset with a vision for the future.

When you first start saving, it won't feel like much money and you may question how your numbers are going to grow. Even after you purchase your first few properties, unless you hit a home run right out of the gate, the needle may not move drastically. The first steps are the most significant, though. The hardest part is to commit and trust that this will work for you.

The concept of not "playing small" sounds like a cliché, and it can feel elusive. But you have to start seeing yourself as a woman who is wealthy—a woman who can do big things! Don't rush this process but continue to do the mindset work as you expand out of your comfort zone.

If you've been struggling and longing for relief from stress over money for so long, it can be hard to know how to be on the other side of it. You might also start to worry about your freedom and contentment. What if you lose it? You may also feel overwhelmed with figuring out how and where to invest more money. Then again, maybe you're thinking you'd *love* to have that problem, or maybe you're already there. It's a good problem to have, but it can still be overwhelming. Wherever you are, keep going back to the steps in this book and practice gratitude, grace and trust in the process. Trust who you are and where you're headed.

I had to go through this process, too. It wasn't easy, and I'm still challenged as I continue to take on larger projects that I'm not sure how to accomplish. I wasn't one of those investors who could dive into 100 units out of the gate. I had to honor my process and my pace, taking the steps that felt comfortable to me. You need to do the same, but as long as you're taking steps, you will keep moving forward.

As I continue to build my wealth and portfolio, more money goes out the door before it comes back in. So until you trust the process and time, you probably won't feel comfortable. It will only be after you repeatedly take action and experience some big wins—while also learning from your losses—that you'll feel like you're living on the other side of progress. If you've come this far in the book, I'm confident that's where you want to be and that you can get there.

Expanding Your Numbers

The money you have coming into your account needs to be logged, and every dollar needs to be accounted for. Often when money comes into our account, we save some for emergencies without creating any long-term savings for money we plan to invest. It's a huge area of finance that many people miss because we aren't taught to have big visions of financial freedom.

This is why most people never get anywhere growing their wealth. It simply won't build if you keep working and working and never put anything aside for investing. The biggest hurdle is that money expands over time, so you won't see a finish line at the outset; this, of course, can make investing scary. But if you follow the guidance I've shared, you'll have a much better chance of living without money worries than if you leave money in your bank account where it will only earn .03%.

The power of time combined with budgeting surpasses any other method for growing wealth. You can build wealth with even a modest salary by investing a small amount each month at 10% interest per year. Shooting for a minimum of 10% a year in real estate is a conservative way to grow your wealth without taking an incredible amount of risk. You just need to take consistent action and let time do its part.

What If You Lose Money?

Yes, you can lose money. But if you're determined and focused, even if you lose some, you'll know more the next time you venture out. Plus, as an asset class, real estate is unlikely to ever drop to zero. Property always has value, especially because we live in a time when housing can't keep up with the demand. At the time of writing this book, it's 2021. With the massive amount of money being printed by the government, the dollar is being devalued, and real estate is a great hedge against inflation. Also, with the high demand for housing and a supply shortage, even if your property value dips for a period of time, it will almost certainly return and surpass that amount in the long run. If you look at the history of real estate, that truth is revealed.

The beauty about building wealth is that time is on your side. As long as you save enough surplus for unforeseen repairs, you can weather almost any storm.

If You Need Money Now

The concept of having to wait to make the money you want may sound frustrating. I frequently hear the complaint about living frugally now so that you can have money later. People have a *carpe diem* attitude and there's nothing wrong with that, but you have to find a balance that works for you. This isn't an either/or scenario. You can certainly spend some of what you have without stressing and can set yourself up to collect cash flow so that you're earning every month.

The bottom line is that if you aren't willing to give something up to get something else, you simply won't have any money left to invest. People sometimes insist that they can't afford to put any money away because they need every cent that they make, but let's consider that seriously. Recently, I started ordering food from a restaurant with a to-go box along with my plate of food. I immediately take food off my plate and place it in the box. When I eat what's on the plate, I'm finished. I trick my mind because I only eat half of the meal. (Then, I have food for the next day.)

You can do the same with money and saving if you live within your means. If you take $100 a month out of your budget, you will learn to live with less. Sometimes people even start to make more because of the psychological impact of taking charge over saving, investing and growing their wealth.

Letting Go of a Limited Mindset

Not putting any money away to build wealth is living with the idea that money is finite rather than abundant. If you're stuck in that mindset, go back and read Chapter 2. You're also not honoring the way money works and how it can work with you and support you if you manage it. If you believe you're capable of earning as much as you want, you won't be so concerned about putting some away because you'll know that you can make more. You'll know that it's you in charge of how you manage money and that you shouldn't be at the mercy of earning a 9-5 living. I'm not claiming this is an easy shift. It took me a long time to get rid of my money baggage, but I'm living proof that it can be done!

Tenant Versus Owner Mentality

Remember: the owner gets someone to pay for their property and gets income monthly to grow wealth. A tenant pays that income and watches the money go out the door every month with nothing to show for it. Why would you want to pay rent your entire life, giving your money away when someone can be paying *you* rent? For people like me who grew up living in an apartment, the tenant mentality was the reality I knew. Mr. Burger, our landlord, was the one who got the money every month while we scraped by. I never thought we could be the landlords!

There are some famous real estate experts like Robert Kiyosaki (author of *Rich Dad, Poor Dad*) who believe buying a home is a bad idea. It's in your liability column because you owe someone money, and money goes out of your account as opposed to into your account every month. I've never agreed with this, because you need to live somewhere, and you have to pay someone rent or a mortgage. But paying for a mortgage is different from paying rent because the money goes toward an asset that you own. Many people who never end up making a ton of money are able to live on the equity from their home or have their home paid off in their aging years.

Granted, this isn't a book about living marginally, and I want you to have more money than you know what to do with. But the point is that I believe your personal home provides pride of ownership, a sense of security and a sound way to build up equity without having to work at it. You want to be the owner not only of your home but of many homes. You want as many people as you can paying you monthly rent.

Tax Advantages

When you buy a property, you aren't just getting the cash flow—you're also getting to write off part of the investment on your taxes by way of depreciation.

Depreciation is calculated based on the lifespan of all parts of the property and allows you to deduct that amount annually. It's similar to the tax deduction you may take for a company car. Your ability to take this deduction will vary depending on whether you're a W-2 earner, a business owner or a real estate professional.

As a professional in the field, bonus depreciation allows people to accelerate the deduction on properties in the first year and take both active and passive losses. Otherwise, you can take passive losses only on passive income. In other words, if you make $20,000 in a syndication and lose $20,000 in the stock market, you'll cancel out your taxes for that year.

You also need to understand that depreciation is a tax deferral, not a one-and-done deduction. In other words, you can take depreciation, but when a property sells, there is a depreciation recapture. Remember that any time you make a profit, Uncle Sam wants his share. The only way to avoid paying is with legal tax strategies continuously implemented. The tax laws can change frequently, so you need a strong CPA on your team to support you with this strategy.

If you actively manage properties for 750 hours a year,

you can qualify as a real estate professional. The advantages to that distinction are great, because you can then take all real estate deductions as a loss. If you have a $200,000 loss, it will offset any other income you or your spouse make. Many investing couples have one W-2 earner and one real estate professional in the family so that they can get loans and deductions. Still, make sure you qualify for real estate professional status before using this strategy, as the government has strict rules since many people want the designation to benefit from tax advantages.

Some CPAs don't have the best strategies for working with tax law or don't understand how to work with real estate deductions, so check the laws yourself as well. Even if you find a CPA you like, if they don't know about tax strategies as your portfolio becomes more complex, find a new one. Otherwise, you're potentially leaving too much money on the table.

Compounding Income

Another advantage you have with real estate is that as your tenants pay your mortgage, your debt decreases. Plus, with inflation, rents tend to increase over time. If you get a 30-year fixed loan, the rents will increase, the value of the property will appreciate and the loan rate will stay locked in. Most people refinance or sell before 30 years which negates the terms of the loan, but it's still a great way to mitigate your risk. So, if you have a $225,000 mortgage, in 10 years, you will only owe $150,000 on that loan. The $75,000 you have paid down is part of your profit!

Passive Investments

To qualify for syndications, you often need to be an accredited investor. This means that you need to have earned $200,000 as a single person or $300,000 as a married couple for the past three years or have $1 million in net worth, minus your primary home. If you know something about investing and have relationships with sponsors, you can get into these kinds of deals with accreditation.

It depends on how a syndication is set up and classified with the United States Securities and Exchange Commission (SEC), which is the federal agency responsible for administering federal security laws that protect investors. The SEC also ensures that security markets are fair and honest.

To find these opportunities, start talking to people who have deals. Listen to podcasts such as *Bigger Pockets*, *The Real Estate InvestHER* or *Cashflow Ninja*. You can also go to meetups and networking events, or you can join the *Bigger Pockets* forum. Even if you find an amazing deal, start small and never put all of your eggs in one basket.

When a deal is offered, you'll be sent a summary with the details, terms and projections. There will be a minimum investment of anywhere from $25,000 to $100,000, and when you're ready, you'll sign the subscription documents. But remember: never sign anything you don't understand. Always ask questions to get clarity.

Once the documents are signed, you'll fund the deal and your sponsor will also sign the documents and return them to you. In the documents, they'll also offer what's known as a preferred return, which is a promise to pay you that amount before they get their cut. It's usually anywhere from 6-8% annualized. On a new purchase, you will likely get that preferred return accrued. This means that although the property will still need some improvements and rent increases before you'll start seeing returns, you will still be paid in the interim. Cash flow payments generally start within six months with the accrued amount from the previous six months factored in.

When you exit the deal, you can expect an additional 10%+ on your money annualized. Hold periods are anywhere from two to 10 years.

Most sponsors will have a portal where you can sign in to check your account. They will also email updates letting you know about improvements that are being made to the investments, finances or sales. Always confirm wire instructions directly with someone at the company for verification.

Additionally, you'll get a tax document called a K-1. This form, depending on your circumstances, may enable you to take depreciation against your other income. Since the properties are often leveraged and the deductions for the improvements are sizable, you can expect to see your portion of the investment participating on paper in those losses.

Like an investment property, you should set up an LLC for your funds—or you can put the investment directly in the name of the trust. Remember that the LLC and the trust are always designed to protect your other assets in the event of a lawsuit.

If you invested through your self-directed IRA, other restrictions will apply. It's important to understand those rules and regulations before investing. Each retirement plan has documents with various restrictions.

Opportunity Zones

An opportunity zone is another great place to put taxable gains for tax benefits. These deals are in areas that the city wants to see built up. If you take taxable gains from a property, you can put them into a deal like this and get your money out in five to 10 years. You will still need to pay taxes on the original investment, but all of the profits will be tax-free.

Creating a Monopoly and Lasting Wealth

You realize by now that there are many ways to make lasting wealth through real estate. You can own many single-family homes and pay the mortgages down monthly. The homes will give you cash flow, are easy to sell and will be paid off over time.

You can also grow wealth through multi-family properties. Many multi-family investors like to buy 100 units or more because they can hire full-time maintenance and managers, which brings down the overhead and bottom-line costs. You can also hire full-time staff to manage four buildings with 25 units each or 100 single-family homes, creating a lot of cash flow in one concentrated place.

You will need to commit to a plan. If you're just starting out and don't have a lot of cash or a high tolerance for risk, find a market where you can afford to buy a property for $100,000 with $20,000 down. You'll need to put money into the investment, manage it and just sit tight. Then, repeat. Whatever deal you find will ideally offer some monthly cash flow as well.

But don't forget that the way wealth builds is through a rinse and repeat process. Eventually, it will become addictive, and you'll start to see more and more opportunities as you dive in deeper.

Chapter 10 Actions:

Let's set your intentions using a five-year plan working backwards:

1. What is your five-year goal?

2. To achieve your goal, what do you need to do in year four?

3. To achieve your goal, what do you need to do in year three?

4. To achieve your goal, what do you need to do in year two?

5. To achieve your goal, what do you need to in year one?

6. What is holding you back? Who can help you?

ELEVEN

THE MILLIONAIRESS MENTALITY

> *If you don't risk anything, you risk even more.*
> —Erica Jong

The key to real estate investing is having a goal in mind and working toward it, knowing that time is always your best friend. It's never too late to start!

My only regret is that I wish I would have been a bold investor sooner. I didn't have the knowledge or know where to get it. Even when I started, I was so scared. I often retreated from investment opportunities that made sense because of the fear of loss and because I didn't trust myself. Then, I felt defeated. Once I started to see that money and my access to it was abundant, I was able to make educated decisions without fear in the way. Eventually, I learned that I couldn't count on every deal being a success, so I discovered that diversification was the winning strategy.

Don't let a lack of money scare you like I let it scare me. Don't worry about the worst-case scenarios, because they rarely ever happen. Even if the market crashes, as long as you can cash flow the property and you have reserves saved up, you'll be fine to ride the wave.

As mentioned previously, 93% of millionaires are made through real estate, and only 30% of them are women. You can be a part of closing that gap. We need to believe that there's enough for everyone and that with more financial resources, we will be able to live a more fulfilling life while providing for our families and for those in need. As soon as you decide to put the brakes on your limited beliefs and break through the mental barriers about what can and can't be done (and what you deserve), a world of abundance will open up to you. Then, you'll begin to make strides.

Financial freedom is possible when you stop believing the lies you've been told about real estate. Don't let yourself think it's the end of the world if you make a mistake. Most successful investors have lost money at one time or another.

What's Stopping You?

Starting from the beginning is always challenging, because it feels like you're never going to get from where you are to where you want to be. But it's proven that if you stay on track, you'll inevitably move forward in real estate —and doing so doesn't have to deplete you of all of your resources or energy.

Every time you think you can't handle it, ask yourself these questions. In fact, answer them right now as you read each one:

1. What's standing in my way?
2. What am I telling myself about my circumstances? Is it fact or fear?
3. Is it truly not possible for me to become a millionairess through real estate?
4. What will financial freedom provide for me?
5. What will it feel like to no longer worry about money or things I don't want to do every day?

Ultimately, what I hope you will find is that the cost of not investing is much greater than taking the chance to dive in. Remember, you aren't alone. There are resources, mentorships and coaches. There are also groups you can join for free (although I caution you not to get all your information for free—we tend to pay more attention and apply ourselves more when we pay for it).

Find Your Financial Freedom Number

I often see clients racing down a road to nowhere when it comes to reaching financial freedom. They feel that no matter how much money they make, there will never be enough. When I ask them for a number that will make them stop worrying about money, they don't have an answer.

Building your portfolio to meet your big picture goals will give you peace of mind as long as you have a number in mind that will be enough.

If you haven't gone through the steps in Chapter 3, please go back and complete that part of this process. The other incredible piece to this exercise is that once you go through the steps to calculate your number, it will be a lot less than you think.

Figuring out a number that enables you to relax about meeting your financial goals is a game changer. It allows you to stop constantly thinking *I have to make more money*. Most women skip this step, and as a result, they're left with a nagging feeling that their life will always be run by the need to make more money.

You've been running at full speed for so long that it feels uncomfortable to take a seat in first class and let someone pour you a drink. Still, getting out of that stuck place isn't that difficult.

Do you need a huge house in an expensive area with a flashy car? Do you love to travel first class? Do you support family members? These are questions you need to ask yourself to come up with your number.

You also need to take taxes into account. For example, if you want $20,000 net per month after taxes, you'll need to earn $30,000 gross or $360,000 per year. If you're currently 40 years old and will live to be 80, you might multiply $360,000 x 40 years to get a total of $14,400,000. Seeing that number, you might think that I am out of my mind, or that saving that much is a lost cause. While I may be a bit out there, the truth is you don't need anywhere near that amount to live comfortably at $20,000 a month, nor do you need to work hard for the rest of your life.

Before you go crazy thinking that even $20,000 a month is a lot of money, remember that at a certain point, generating that much every month isn't that difficult. That's because as your portfolio builds and generates passive income, your net worth builds, too—and at a certain point, it becomes self-sustaining.

Let's say you build up to $5 million worth of real estate and you're making 10% a year on that money. That would be worth $500,000 a year, which is $41,666 a month in passive income ($500,000 divided by 12).

With that amount of passive income coming in, even if you spent 7.5% of your net worth annually in expenses, you would still be net positive and your money would compound. In other words, with $5 million in base net worth, your passive income would continue to generate earnings without lowering your net worth after the first year, even with expenses factored in—and in five years, it would even exceed your original balance!

This example is easier to see with some simplified accounting, which I've done below:

Year 1:
Expenses: $5,000,000 - $360,000 (-7.5%) = $4,640,000

Year 2:
Interest: $4,640,000 + $464,000 (10%) = $5,104,000
Expenses: $5,104,000 - $382,800 (-7.5%) = $4,721,200

Year 3:
Interest: $4,721,000 + $472,000 (10%) = $5,193,000
Expenses: $5,193,000 - $389,000 (-7.5%) = $4,804,000

Year 4:
Interest: $4,804,000 + $480,800 (10%) = $5,284,800
Expenses: $5,284,800 - $396,000 (-7.5%) = $4,887,700

Year 5:
Interest: $4,887,700 + $488,000 (10%) = $5,374,000

Remember that this is without counting in any tax savings and only considers you living off your passive income. Also, these numbers are close approximations based on your spending and interest earned annually (it is impossible to precisely calculate because the figures will fluctuate based on how much you spend or save in any given month). The point is to see how your passive income replenishes your $5 million—do you see how your money can work for you instead of the other way around?

These numbers may seem high or low to you; it's all relative. But it's easy to see that you don't need to get to $14 million to generate the income you want so you can live an extravagant life. Your numbers may be a lot higher or lower than mine, but I assure you, they aren't as hard to reach as you think—especially if you keep breaking down your goals. The finish line is financial freedom, and knowing where you're headed makes it more likely you'll get there.

Don't forget your initial calculations once you've created them. I recommend checking every few months on how you're progressing toward your big vision goals. Even if the numbers feel elusive to you at this point, push through the exercise and write something down anyway. It's likely that as you progress on your journey, your numbers will get larger.

Getting Yourself Out of the Rat Race Trap

Since you're reading this book, you're already in the minority for simply declaring that you want more money. It isn't easy because we aren't taught it's okay to want it, or that we can have it. On the one hand, "life is hard" is an all-too-common phrase; on the other, when we stop thinking that way, we start judging ourselves and others for being lazy and not living large enough.

There needs to be a point where you decide you no longer have anything to prove and you're satisfied with your accomplishments. There needs to be a point when you acknowledge you've reached the finish line. Then, as long as you're enjoying the fruits of your labor and planning to secure your finances for future generations, you can work on a new business that inspires you. You can spend time volunteering for charities or traveling. You can continue to invest passively and enjoy watching the money roll in without much effort.

Make a commitment to enjoy your time and acknowledge how far you've come. Even if you aren't there yet, celebrate your small wins.

Also, remember it's okay to hit a milestone and realize you want to expand, or to acknowledge that you were playing a lot smaller in the past and are now capable of greater things. As your success and mindset grow, so does your appetite for achieving bigger goals and dreams. It's fine to expand as long as it's coming from enjoying the growth and not from a feeling of scarcity, panic or stress over not having enough.

Parting Words

In addition to all of the perks of growing a real estate portfolio, investing is fun and addictive. If you like people, it's a very interactive business that includes working with partners and team members. If you like being creative, there's so much room to innovate, expand and design.

Becoming a millionaire is less about having a specific amount of money in your bank account than it is about what that money can provide for you. You need to decide how you're going to spend and invest your dollars so that they can multiply. Becoming a millionaire takes conscious effort, and those who are thoughtful about building wealth and living abundantly are more likely to enjoy the fruits of their efforts.

As for me, I prioritized wealth, took logical chances and lived within my means even as I made more money. Before I knew it, my bank account was stacked. Today, I live in a nice home and spend my days helping women and couples grow their wealth through real estate while I continue to invest. My investments support my lifestyle whether I work or not. My husband and kids are thriving, healthy and happy. I travel when I want and wherever I want. My life is by my own design. I also have time to expand my world beyond me. I can focus on making the world a better place and contribute time and money towards that end. It is a rewarding feeling.

Don't settle for a mediocre life. You deserve more, and real estate will give you access to that life. Stay focused and keep yourself accountable. Recommit again and again to what you want for yourself. Reset your money fear barometer and take care of your body and mind so that you can get up again and again when you fall. Keep buying real estate, and you too will develop the Millionairess Mentality.

I'm thrilled you've made it to the end of the book. By now, your mind is no doubt racing with ideas.

Can you do me a favor? I poured my heart and soul into this book, and it would mean the world to me if you emailed me some feedback at hello@wealthbuilding-concierge.com. Otherwise, you can find me on Instagram @wealthbuildingconcierge.

ACKNOWLEDGMENTS

I set out to write this book because I realized it would be something that would live beyond me. In 50 years, this book will still be able to inspire women to get on the path to wealth.

While I'm grateful to myself for stepping up to live a life of freedom, it wouldn't be as doable without my partner and rock of 25 years, Matt Earl Beesley. He has stood by my side and supported me to grow as big as I can imagine.

I'm thankful for those who have supported me as I refined this book's vision, messaging and writing—including Melanie Votaw, Michelle Lewis, Avery Carl, Kristin Marquet and Anna David.

A big thank you to my real estate investing mentors and dear friends, Justin Donald, Derek Graham, David Lawver, Julie Gates and Lowie Van Diest.

This book would not have been written without the love and encouragement of my soul sister, Tammy Randall Wood, who inspires me to shine brightly in the world every day.

Lastly, I'm forever appreciative of GoBundance Women and my tribe of sisters who support me and cheer me on with more love than I could ever have dreamed possible.

ABOUT THE AUTHOR

Tamar Hermes is the CEO of Wealth Building Concierge, a company committed to helping professional women and couples across the country manage their money and grow wealth. She spends her days doing what she loves: coaching and investing, confident in her knowledge that her money will continue to build through her investments —whether or not she works a traditional job. Tamar is committed to helping women understand how to grow wealth beyond their wildest dreams by first building a firm financial foundation. Her vision is to help every woman make life choices based on their personal passions, and not solely on the need to make money.

Currently, Tamar lives in Austin, Texas with her husband, two children and her sweet terrier, Teena. You can find her walking by Ladybird Lake, cruising the city on her electric bike or dining with friends at one of the countless amazing restaurants in town. She is also an avid traveler. If you have any great vacation ideas, please e-mail them to hello@wealthbuildingconcierge.com.

CPSIA information can be obtained
at www.ICGtesting.com
Printed in the USA
BVHW040802080522
636222BV00052B/632